THE VOYAGES OF
COLUMBUS

1492–1504

"There will a come a time in future ages when the ocean will loosen the chains of the universe and a vast land will appear, new worlds will be seen and Iceland will not be the end of the earth."
– Seneca, *Medea*

Next to these lines, which Columbus knew, his son Fernando wrote in Latin: "This prophecy was fulfilled by my father, Admiral Christopher Columbus, in the year 1492."

LORENZO CAMUSSO

THE VOYAGES
OF
COLUMBUS
1492–1504

Dorset Press
New York

ENDPAPERS
This late-16th-century map of the Caribbean, the continental coast, and the Antilles – the seas and lands explored by Columbus – is by Theodor de Bry. Around 1570, this Dutch artist established his own engraving workshop in Frankfurt. Beginning in 1590, he started publishing illustrated descriptions of late 15th- and 16th-century voyages. This map, as well as other illustrations in the following pages, is a selection taken from de Bry's 27 published volumes. The Latin captions identify many of the places discovered by Columbus during his four voyages.

Copyright © 1991 by Arnoldo Mondadori Editore, S.p.A., Milan

English translation copyright © 1991 by Arnoldo Mondadori Editore, S.p.A., Milan

English translation by Elizabeth Leister

Art Director: Fulvio Ariani
Editor: Franca Cambiè
Maps: Studio Dream, Verona
Editorial Project: Fenice 2000 S.r.l., Milan

First published in the U.S.A. by Dorset Press, a division of Marboro Books Corp.

ISBN 0–88029–707–7

Printed and bound in Italy by Arnoldo Mondadori, Verona

At right, the town of Angra on the Island of Terceira in the Azores. Museu di Marinha, Lisbon.

Contents

The 15th-Century European World

·

*How travelers and trade routes linked Europe and Asia * Myths, superstitions, and Marco Polo * The Great Debate: How big is the world? * The theories of Aristotle and Ptolemy*

Leaves and fruit of the nutmeg (right) and harvesting pepper (below), from an illustration in a French edition of Marco Polo's story. These were two of the most important Oriental spices, and were in great demand by 15th-century Europeans. By Columbus' time the spice trade had become a major industry – large, profitable, and truly international.

When Christopher Columbus was still a boy playing in the streets of Genoa, men regularly sailed from Portugal to the Azores, a chain of islands well out into the Atlantic Ocean, nearly a third of the way to Maryland. They sailed confidently to Iceland and to the Cape Verde Islands off the western coast of Africa. But there were men who also believed that somewhere on earth there was an Earthly Paradise, closed off by gates of crystal and fire. From this paradise flowed the great rivers: the Ganges and the Nile, the Tigris and the Euphrates.

During this period, Europe was linked to the Orient by a thriving international trade network that brought back spices and stories from the Molucca Islands in Indonesia. But few Europeans actually reached these far-off lands.

The geographical knowledge of the Middle Ages is summed up in mappa mundi – *maps of the world – like the one above, which was made in Spain around the year 1375. Only the Mediterranean is recognizable and clearly defined; everything else fades into vague uncertainty. Some elements of this map are totally imaginary – for example, the crescent-shaped land, a sort of appendix to Africa, south of the present-day Gulf of Guinea. The three parts of the then-known world – Europe, Africa, and Asia – were believed to be surrounded by a single ocean. Its size was a subject of debate among geographers – or "cosmographers," as they were called – who sought the answers in the writings of Greek and Roman authorities. Columbus' momentous voyage replaced speculation with exploration; until then, however, the unknown had no dimensions.*

The most famous European traveler, of course, was Marco Polo, who wrote an account – part fact, part fantasy – about his journey to China. Marco Polo's journal was not a factual historical document; it was entertaining, and it surely encouraged further

speculation about mysterious lands and faraway places.

In the 15th century, there was not always a clear separation between literary image and geographical fact. In the vast uncharted oceans that surrounded the known land masses – Europe, Africa, Asia – maybe there really *were* fearsome whirlpools, and giant sea monsters, and magnetic reefs that could pull iron nails out of ships' hulls.

To be sure, many superstitions and myths from earlier ages had already been discredited. Educated Europeans knew that the world was round, and they were aware that Portuguese voyagers to the African

tropics had seen many people and lush vegetation in the Torrid Zone which ancient writers had described as uninhabitable.

Still, most of the earth's geography, and even the precise outlines of Europe itself, was a mystery in the 15th century. Most "experts" based their view of the world on the opinions of Greek and

15th-century Portuguese sailors expanded the horizons of the known world, but the Ocean was still a great mystery. Many people believed that monstrous creatures, like the one pictured below, lurked in its uncharted depths.

Roman writers. In medieval times, the prevailing authority was Aristotle. In his opinion, which was shared by Roman writers such as Seneca and Pliny, the earth's land surface was extremely vast, and only a narrow sea separated Europe and Asia.

But the Aristotelian view was directly challenged at the

Ancient scholars knew that the world was round, and so did 15th-century Europeans. Their belief was confirmed by classical writings, and also by experience. As can be seen from this 15th-century drawing, Columbus' contemporaries had observed that objects "sink" over the horizon as a result of the curvature of the earth.

beginning of the 15th century. Renaissance scholars rediscovered the writings of Ptolemy, the Greek astronomer and geographer who lived in the 2nd century A.D. His treatise on geography was translated into Latin, the universal language of the time, and his ideas – and the ideas of his Arab sources – became widely known. According to Ptolemy, the earth's surface was equally divided between land and water, and his followers believed that a vast, impassable ocean extended westwards from Europe to the Far East.

Columbus questioned the teachings of Ptolemy. He believed the ocean *could* be crossed. But neither he, nor Aristotle, nor Ptolemy guessed a huge undiscovered continent lay between Europe and the Orient.

1451
The Man from Genoa

·

*Columbus' Italian ancestry * His boyhood
* Genoa's important role in the 15th-
century seafaring world*

The Lavagna, a stream in the northern Italian region of Liguria, flows through a valley called Fontanabuona, just behind the eastern Riviera. It mixes with other streams to form the Entella River, which empties into the sea between the towns of Chiavari and Lavagna. Without doubt, Columbus' roots were in this valley of Fontanabuona, a land of hillside farms and slate quarries. His grandfather Giovanni came from Moconesi, one of the small towns in the valley, and he later moved to Quinto, a nearby coastal village five miles from the center of Genoa. Giovanni had a son, Domenico, who was sent to Genoa as a weaver's

Genoa as it appears in Michael Wolgemut's woodcut, from The Book of Chronicles (1493). It is the first printed view of the city. The concise drawing is stylized in a typically medieval fashion, but it includes some precise details – for example, the two lighthouses in the port, the parallel piers jutting out from the eastern shore, and the Castelletto.

apprentice. Domenico became a tavernkeeper and the proprietor of a weaving shop. He eventually was to own two houses and some fields. The dowry of his wife, Susanna Fontanarossa, included some land holdings. Susanna and Domenico had at least five children:

Giovanni Pellegrino, who died young; Bartolomeo; Diego; Bianchetta, who married one Giacomo Bavarello, the son of a cheesemaker; and Cristoforo ("Christopher"). Domenico Columbus lived to be an old man, perhaps until the age of 80 – an extraordinarily long life by 15th-century standards. His name lives on in the New World: the capital of today's Dominican Republic is called Santo Domingo after the patron saint of the man whose son discovered this Caribbean island.

Records of Christopher's birth either do not exist, or their whereabouts is unknown. But it can be deduced from other documents that he was born in 1451, between the end of August and the end of October. In all likelihood, Columbus was born either in a house on Vico dell'Olivella in Genoa, or in the house in Quinto belonging to his grandfather, where it would have been customary for his

mother to have returned to give birth.

When Christopher was not yet four years old, his father moved his house and shop to the Sant'Andrea district of

At right and below, two details from a late-sixteenth-century painting by Cristoforo de' Grassi, depicting the city of Genoa. It is an accurate copy of an older painting, and faithfully represents the city as it was in 1481.

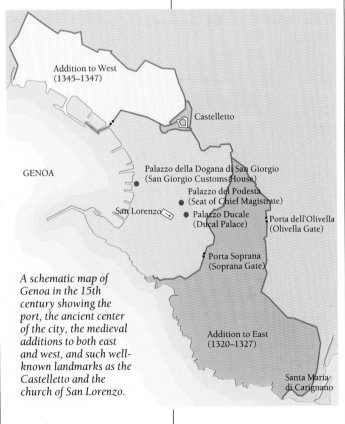

A schematic map of Genoa in the 15th century showing the port, the ancient center of the city, the medieval additions to both east and west, and such well-known landmarks as the Castelletto and the church of San Lorenzo.

Genoa. The property had a garden behind, and was situated between the street and the city walls. On the ground floor was the weaving shop, upstairs the family rooms. In modern-day Genoa there is a street called Vico Diritto, and one of the dwellings there is known as the Columbus house. It is possible that it was indeed this house where Christopher spent his childhood.

In those days, Italy was a collection of city-states bound together – and divided – by political alliances and family ties. Genoa was one of the most important city-states, largely because its strategic location on the Mediterranean coast made it an important center of trade and finance.

Two rival groups, the Adorno and Fregoso families, fought bitterly for control of the city. The Adornos were supported by the rulers of Aragon in Spain; the Fregosos, with whom Columbus' father sided, were backed by the house of Anjou in France. The two sides opposed each other at every turn. Spanish and French

The Columbus house in Moconesi, a small town in the Ligurian valley of Fontanabuona.

The Legino house near Savona, about 30 miles (50 km) from Genoa. Domenico Columbus moved here when Christopher was in his teens.

armies and fleets sometimes passed through Genoa, adding to the turmoil. Local rulers, called doges, were made and unmade as the balance of power shifted back and forth.

In 1463, when Christopher Columbus was 12 years old, Archbishop Paolo Fregoso regained the title of doge after it had been wrested away for a brief period. Pope Pius II wrote to him, marveling that he had consented to govern the city that "more than any other in Italy delights in new things, that is always changing and is always in motion." But the Archbishop's rule was short-lived: the following year Francesco Sforza, the Duke of Milan, took control of the city.

When Constantinople was conquered by the Turks in 1453, some of Genoa's trade bases in the Middle East were cut off and its interests in that

region were threatened. But Genoa remained a major force. When the city's Senate asked Francesco Sforza for his protection, its members were able to boast that their territorial possessions included the Rivieras, Corsica, the Greek islands of Lesbos, Khíos and Thásos, Famagusta on Cyprus, Kaffa, and other important trading centers on the Black Sea.

This was the Genoa into which Christopher Columbus was born in 1451. No later than 1470, when he was 19, his father appears to have moved the family to Savona, further west on the coast. By then Christopher had already found his sea legs and, no doubt, had begun to dream of distant voyages like the one that would one day make him the most famous mariner of all time.

Mythological Ancestors and Birthplaces

15th- and 16th-century historians were correct in saying that Columbus was born in Genoa and then left his homeland, first for Portugal then for Spain. But as the centuries passed and Columbus' fame diminished – for that is what happened – these facts were disputed and many absurd claims were made. For instance, a book published in London in 1682 says in all innocence that Columbus was "born in England, but lived in Genoa." In 1687, a French lawyer named Jean Colomb claimed that the discoverer of the New World was his countryman and ancestor. These confusing claims reached their height around 1892, the fourth centennial of America's discovery.

Over the years, a number of people have claimed Columbus as their direct ancestor. There was a Portuguese Columbus, a nobleman who fled to Genoa and returned home with an Italian name; a Greco-French pirate known as Coulon; another claimant born in Spanish Plasencia; another in Spanish Tortosa. Even a Swiss citizen, a certain Mr. Colomb who was friendly with Italian expatriots, insisted that the famous navigator was his ancestor.

It seems Columbus also had many birthplaces. A number of small towns on Italy's Ligurian coast claim him as their native son. There is a tombstone in the Corsican town of Calvi, a 15th-century Genoese stronghold, that makes the same claim. And there are some who believe that Columbus was indeed from Genoa, but was descended from a family of Spanish Jews. This last claim has never been proven true or false; like many aspects of Columbus' life, it remains a subject of conjecture.

A Man of the Sea

•

*Columbus' early years * Sailor, student, or merchant? * Two Mediterranean voyages * Columbus fights a sea battle, marries, and settles in Portugal * His voyage to Africa*

"*De muy pequeña hedad entré en la mar navegando, e lo he continuado hasta hoy.*" So wrote Columbus in a letter to the royal family of Spain: "I began sailing at a very early age and have continued doing so up to the present day." His second child and biographer, Fernando Columbus, says that "when my father was quite young he learned his letters, and in Pavia he studied as much as he needed to understand cosmography." And in a legal document dated 1472, Christopher, who was 21 at the time, is called *lanerius* – that is, a wool merchant like his father Domenico.

These three biographical fragments – our only clues to Columbus' youth – present a confusing picture. Was the young Columbus a sailor, as he himself says; or a university student, as his son implies; or a wool merchant, as the public records indicate?

It is hard to imagine Columbus spending his formative years poring over books in the halls of the distinguished university in

Pavia. It seems likely that Fernando Columbus mixed up his father's reminiscences, and that Christopher's formal education – including the study of "cosmography" or geography – took place on the Vicolo Pavia in Genoa, where the wool merchant's guild had its own elementary school for the children of the master weavers.

As for his being a "wool merchant," this description of the 21-year-old Columbus probably means that his first sea voyages were in some way connected with his father's business of buying wool or selling cloth. Or it could mean that, like other mariners at the time, he sought out or accepted small shipments of trade goods in order to scrape together some money.

This was the normal procedure for learning about the business of seafaring in 15th-century Genoa. At the time, the city's economic empire was held together by a vast network of

An old view of the city and island of Scio, or Khíos as it is called today, off the coast of Turkey. It was a Genoese possession until 1566 when it was conquered for the Turks by Piali Pasha. Columbus was 23 or 24 years old when he visited it on what was almost certainly his first long voyage.

Another view of Genoa by Cristoforo de' Grassi. Large ships are moored in the shelter of the eastern wharf. The derrick at the far end of the wharf indicates that work is in progress to extend it.

Mediterranean trade routes. Later in his life, Columbus refers with familiarity to the ports of Naples in southern Italy, and to Marseilles and Hyères in France. No doubt he sailed to these and other Mediterranean trading ports during his early years, and during these travels began to refine the nautical skills and knowledge that one day would carry him across the Atlantic.

Columbus was 41 years old when he set out on his great voyage of discovery in 1492. He had spent the

previous eight or nine years in a frustrating effort to secure financial backing, first from the king of Portugal and then from the rulers of Spain. But the dates of his first voyage and of his first command are unknown. Many years later, in the logbook of his first trans-Atlantic voyage, Columbus wrote that "*Vi todo el Levante y Poniente*" – "I saw the whole East and West" of the Mediterranean. But in actual fact, only two fairly certain events are known: a voyage to Khíos and a crossing to the Gulf of Tunis.

Khíos, or Scio as it was then called, is one of the Sporades Islands, very near the coast of Turkey. It was a Genoese possession from the beginning of the 14th century, an idyllic island surrounded by deep blue

waters and clear skies, and perfumed with the scent of evergreen thickets and Middle-Eastern spices. In 1474 and 1475 Genoa sent two convoys there. Columbus, who was 23 or 24 at the time, was present on one of these voyages, perhaps the first which left from Savona where his father then lived. This was his first long voyage. It was as close as he ever managed to come to Asia, which in later years he tried to reach by sailing to the west.

The voyage to the Gulf of

Above, a typical Mediterranean port in Columbus' time, from a contemporary Italian illustration.

Tunis, off the coast of North Africa, was a privateering episode that took place during a period of hostilities between René of Anjou, French pretender to the throne of Naples, and the Aragons of Spain. (As noted previously, Christopher's father was allied with the Genoese faction that favored the French.) The event probably occurred in 1475 or 1476. It is described by Columbus in a letter he wrote in 1495, which survives today in the version appearing in the biography written by his son Fernando. The episode sheds light on Columbus' character, and on the seafaring practices of the time.

Columbus was commissioned by René of Anjou to attempt a surprise attack on a large Spanish galley called the Fernandina. On the island of San Pietro, off the coast of Sardinia, he learned that the galley was sailing in a convoy with three

Below, a nautical document from the time when Christopher Columbus was perfecting his knowledge as a seaman: a galley and a round ship under Portuguese flag. (Detail of a map, from 1482, by Grazioso Benincasa.)

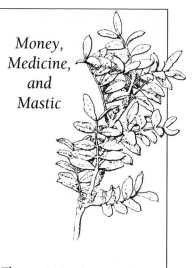

Money, Medicine, and Mastic

The mastic tree is common on the shores of the Mediterranean, and in the southern part of the Aegean island of Khíos there is a particular variety prized for its resin, which was praised for its medicinal properties as long ago as the first century A.D. by Dioscorides, a Greek physician. It made a great impression on Columbus when, at the age of 23 or 24, he saw it on Khíos. Years later, he believed he had discovered mastic in the New World, and thought "it could be traded well right on the spot, without having to bring it back to Spain, selling it to the Great Khan's cities which will undoubtedly be discovered."

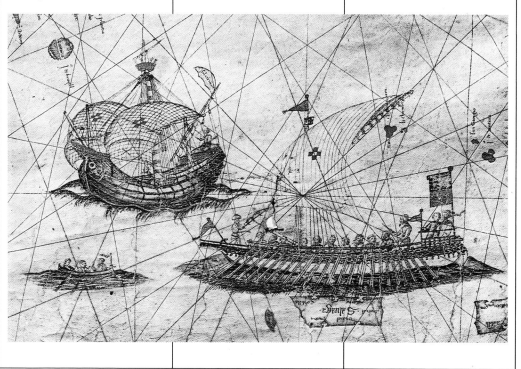

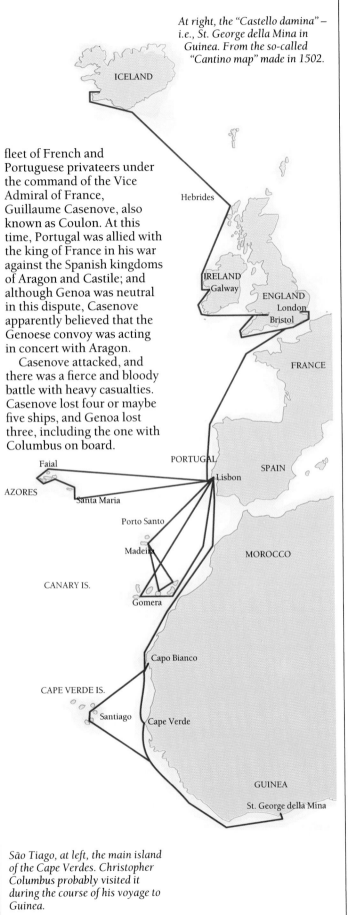

At right, the "Castello damina" – i.e., St. George della Mina in Guinea. From the so-called "Cantino map" made in 1502.

fleet of French and Portuguese privateers under the command of the Vice Admiral of France, Guillaume Casenove, also known as Coulon. At this time, Portugal was allied with the king of France in his war against the Spanish kingdoms of Aragon and Castile; and although Genoa was neutral in this dispute, Casenove apparently believed that the Genoese convoy was acting in concert with Aragon.

Casenove attacked, and there was a fierce and bloody battle with heavy casualties. Casenove lost four or maybe five ships, and Genoa lost three, including the one with Columbus on board.

Above, a map dated somewhere between 1488 and 1493 with all the ports known to Columbus before the voyages of discovery. Some scholars attribute the map to Columbus himself.

At left, a 17th-century print of the city of Angra do Heroísmo on the island of Terceira in the Azores.

commercial expedition bound for England presented Columbus with the opportunity to leave the Mediterranean. He embarked on one of the five ships in the convoy. On August 13, 1476, while on course to round Cape St. Vincent near the southwestern tip of Portugal, the squadron encountered a

other ships. Dismayed by this unexpected news, Columbus' crew wanted to return to Marseilles for reinforcements. Columbus pretended to agree. They sailed all night and "at sunrise," he wrote, "we found ourselves at the Cape of Carthage" instead of Marseilles. Columbus had fooled his men: instead of heading for the safety of Marseilles under the cover of darkness, he had set his course for the Spanish squadron. As this story shows, Columbus by the age of 24 or 25 was a bold and clever veteran who already knew how to command both men and ships.

In 1476, a Genoese

São Tiago, at left, the main island of the Cape Verdes. Christopher Columbus probably visited it during the course of his voyage to Guinea.

The African coast with the Canary and Cape Verde Islands, from a nautical map made in 1516, now in Portugal. His voyages to these Atlantic islands gave Columbus a knowledge of the prevailing wind systems, knowledge that was vital to the success of his later trans-Atlantic crossings.

Construction of the fort began in 1482 and Columbus saw it either that same year or the following one. At the time of Columbus' visit, La Mina – i.e., "the mine" – was yielding 1,700 pounds (800 kilos) of gold per year, and the most likely purpose of his trip was to trade for gold with the local population.

As an important member of the Genoese merchant community in Lisbon, Columbus was probably familiar, before 1492, with the other Atlantic islands. In fact, the evidence suggests that during these years Columbus sailed to Ireland, the Canaries, the Azores, and the Cape Verdes, which he probably visited on his way back from Guinea.

Clinging to an oar, Columbus escaped and swam to shore. Somehow he made his way to Lisbon, the capital of Portugal.

So it was that Columbus arrived in Portugal, where six or seven years later King João II would consider Columbus' plan to sail west to the Indies. By then, Columbus would be a navigator with considerable experience to his credit, a seaman who had explored the known limits of the Atlantic Ocean – from Iceland to Guinea, from Lisbon to the Azores. But for now, Columbus was merely a shipwrecked sailor trying to salvage what he could from an unlucky commercial venture.

The two surviving Genoese ships left Spain, where they had taken refuge in the harbor of Cadiz. Sailing on to Lisbon, they again met up with Casenove. Sheltered in the Portuguese harbor, the same people who had fought each other so ferociously now treated each other with cordial respect. The French Admiral even proposed that the ships from Genoa travel with him in convoy, but the Genoese decided in the end to make their own way to London and Bristol, and Columbus left Portugal on a

The cartographic sketch on the adjacent page summarizes Christopher Columbus' early Atlantic voyages – practically from the Arctic Circle to the Equator – before he presented King João II of Portugal with his plan to reach Asia by sailing west.

British ship.

Columbus eventually returned to Lisbon, where he later married and established a household in Porto Stefano, an island in the Atlantic less than 30 miles (48 km) from Madeira. In July of 1478, Columbus sailed to Madeira, which had been "rediscovered" by the Portuguese in 1420, to buy sugar on behalf of the Di Negro family. Sugarcane had been introduced to the island from Sicily half a century before. This excellent Madeiran sugar was just beginning to gain favor in the European market. However, the business deal in which Columbus was involved was not a success, and ended up in court.

It is certain that during these years Columbus also sailed to Guinea, on the west coast of Africa. There he visited the fortress of St. George della Mina, which belonged to the king of Portugal.

At right, the Hastings Manuscript, a valuable document on seamanship dating from the time of Columbus. Some English ships are anchored; others maneuver in a natural harbor. A very interesting detail (bottom left) is the rudimentary lighthouse consisting of a fire at the top of a wooden trestle.

What Kind of Man Was Columbus?

•

*His appearance and character * How he was described by men who knew him * How artists imagined him*

Another of the most frequently reproduced portraits of Columbus. Painted, as were all known portraits, after the navigator's death, it is not known how close it comes to his true appearance. Below at right, a depiction of Columbus drawn purely from imagination.

"In Genoa, an ancient and noble Italian city, was born Christopher Columbus, son of common people, and as is the custom in Genoa, he went to sea." Everything that has been said

Below, the so-called "Gioviano" portrait of Columbus, probably the oldest of the many pictures of the explorer.

so far about the man from Genoa is incisively summed up in this short sentence from *Navigations and Voyages*, a 16th-century anthology compiled by Giovanni Battista Ramusio. Specifically, this sentence appears at the beginning of *The New World*, a treatise by Pietro Martire d'Anghiera, a native of the Italian town of Arona. Pietro, who had lived

for some time at the Spanish court, provides an important record of how Spain established its American empire during the period 1492–1525, and he also tells us that Columbus was "a man of tall stature, energetic, with ruddy coloring and a good complexion."

The known portraits of Columbus are of little or no help in fleshing out Pietro Martire's description. The Chicago Exposition of 1893, held one year after the 400th anniversary of Columbus' discovery, gathered together 71 portraits – all of them supposedly accurate renderings of the Captain General. But a special commission concluded that none of the portraits was genuine.

One of the most famous portraits is the so-called "Gioviano." It is named after Paolo Giovio, a well-known 16th-century Italian doctor, historian and bishop who commissioned this portrait to hang in his villa along with pictures of other renowned men. The "Gioviano" Columbus appears stern, tired, thinning at the temples,

and perhaps a little flabby. This must be the 49-year-old Columbus who returned, disillusioned and in chains, from his third voyage to America. The "Talleyrand portrait," attributed to Sebastiano del Piombo, shows a face with somewhat coarse features, but full of energy.

Contemporary descriptions of Columbus are remarkably similar. Angelo Trevisan, a Venetian ambassador to Spain, wrote a letter in 1501 referring to his "very great friendship" with Columbus, and describing him as "a man

of very tall stature, ruddy, greatly talented, with a long face." Another reliable description comes from Gonzalo Fernández de Oviedo y Valdés, who was a page at the Spanish court

conventional remarks with comments that seem based on first-person observation. "He was a very reasonable man," writes Oviedo, "cautious and quite clever, a fine man of letters and an extremely learned cosmographer, gracious when he wished and hot-headed in anger."

His contemporaries agree that Columbus possessed great tenacity, fierce pride, courage, a sharp eye and a quick wit. Some speak of his fascinating charm with

The portrait at left seems to be derived from the "Gioviano," so called because it was commissioned by Paolo Giovio, an Italian man of letters.

been influenced by too much sympathy – or in some cases dislike – for Columbus. But history demands that we try to see his actions and behavior objectively, and within the context of his times. For example, it must never be forgotten that Columbus was, as Oviedo points out, a man

when Columbus returned triumphant in 1493 from his first successful trans-Atlantic voyage. Oviedo witnessed Columbus' royal audience in Barcelona, and in his *History of the Indies* describes Columbus as "a well-built man of good stature and of candid appearance. He was taller than average, with strong limbs. He had lively eyes and his features were well proportioned. He had reddish hair and a somewhat flushed, blotchy face."

For additional details, we can turn to *The History of the*

Life and Feats of Christopher Columbus, the biography written by his son Fernando. "The Admiral was a well formed man of more than average stature," writes Fernando, "with a long face, somewhat high cheeks, tending neither towards fat nor lean. He had an aquiline nose, light eyes, fair and flushed with vivid color. In his youth he had blond hair, but when he reached the age of thirty, it became completely white."

As for Columbus' character, Oviedo mixes

women, but this appears to be hearsay; there is no firm evidence that he was – or, for that matter, was not – a ladies' man. As for his nautical skill, Pietro Martire d'Anghiera speaks for many when he writes that Columbus was "the most experienced and surest sea captain of his time."

The judgments of modern biographers have perhaps

An example of Columbus' writing; it is an order for payment. Beneath the complicated initials, it bears the words el almirante *("the admiral").*

Above, the so-called Talleyrand portrait. It is usually considered to be the work of Sebastiano del Piombo.

"of honest parentage" – in other words, a man of middle-class origins, not a nobleman. Yet this son of Genoa was a born leader, equally intrepid in the presence of royalty and of physical danger. He was, in short, a charismatic man who inspired loyalty and steadfast dedication, and his accomplishments reveal his character as clearly as any historical document.

1482

The Path to China

·

*Reasons why Columbus thought he could reach Asia by sailing west * An expert's opinion * How Columbus miscalculated the earth's size*

I n *The History of the Catholic Sovereigns*, Andrés Bernáldez, a priest who befriended Columbus, uses the words *el fecho de su imaginación* – "the fruit of his imagination" – to describe Columbus' plan to reach Asia by sailing west. Columbus' son Fernando also speaks of "imagination" in the formulation of his father's great plan. And while no one knows for certain how and

Below, Toscanelli's concept of geography, with Asia near the Canary islands, is compared with reality.

when Columbus first arrived at the idea of sailing westward to the Orient, we can guess the source of his inspiration.

The idea almost certainly takes shape as he sails the Atlantic as a young man. He sees the color of many skies reflected in its waves, and observes the regularity of its tides. He is an experienced seaman who scoffs at medieval tall-tales. There are no sea monsters. There are no ship-eating magnetic reefs. The torrid zone is not impassable, and

people live below the equator. Columbus has sailed the ocean from Iceland to Guinea (which he mistakenly thinks is south of the equator); why not sail further west, to the land of Genghis Khan?

This train of thought is encouraged by what his son later called "indications," signs that other lands exist to

the west. Other sailors report elusive lands seen like mirages when sailing towards the setting sun, unusual wooden objects found at sea, and trunks of pine trees that the west wind carried to the

This is a reconstruction of the map which Toscanelli sent to the King of Portugal.

shores of the Azores. And then there are two boats, with two strange corpses, found adrift off the shore of Ireland. (The bodies may have been Laplanders, but they were believed to be Chinese.)

These "indications" and his own experience led Columbus to the conclusion that there are lands to the west, and that they must be part of Asia: India, famed for its spices, and Cipango (Japan), and Marco Polo's fabulous Cathay. (However, Columbus may not have read the story of Marco Polo's travels yet. His copy, with its 366 handwritten notes in the margin, was printed in 1485 – long after Columbus' plan was conceived.)

But how to reach those far-

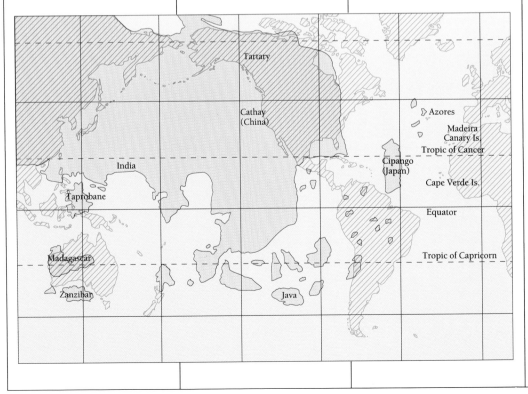

off lands? In an effort to answer this question, Columbus sought the advice of Paolo del Pozzo Toscanelli, a learned Florentine scientist described by the German astronomer

A sea monster attacks a ship. In reality, whenever Columbus' project was considered, the debate focused on the distance and duration of the trip, not on frightening fables.

Johann Müller as the most distinguished mathematician of the time. Columbus wrote to Toscanelli, and received in reply a brief, graceful letter. (It began, "I understand your grand and noble desire to cross to where the spices grow.") Toscanelli also enclosed copies of a letter and map sent a few years earlier (1474) to canon Fernando Martins. The documents were originally meant for King Alfonso V of

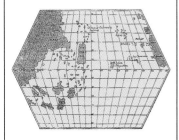

more than 2,400 nautical miles (4,400 km). No wonder he set sail so confidently on his first voyage of discovery: both his calculations and Toscanelli's suggested that sailing from Europe to the Orient was no longer than sailing from Portugal to Guinea, a distance that an

Below, a portrait of the learned Florentine Paolo del Pozzo Toscanelli, and, below left, a reconstruction of Toscanelli's map, centered on the broad ocean between Europe and Asia.

Portugal, who had inquired about the shortest route from Europe to the Indies.

Thus, the seaman who had sailed "everything that up until then had ever been sailed," as he later declared, but who was a self-taught geographer, received the final stimulus to act. The man who epitomized Florentine scientific thought, the most advanced of the time, had confirmed his intuitions. Yes, answered Toscanelli, there were lands to the west, the Indies. The distance from the Canaries to Cipango (Japan) was 3,000 nautical miles (5,500 km), and the navigation was perfectly feasible.

Later, Columbus would reach the conclusion that the distance was even less – no

experienced captain could easily traverse.

In reality, Columbus grossly underestimated the distance. The actual distance from the Canary Islands to Asia was more than four times what he thought – a total of 10,600 nautical miles (19,600 km).

A Mysterious Pilot

What inspired Columbus to think that he could reach new lands by sailing west? This question has preoccupied modern historians as well as Columbus' contemporaries, some of whom were reluctant to admit that this stubborn, self-assured man from Genoa had been right and that his successful voyage had proven the point in a simple, straightforward manner.

Inevitably, some people believed that Columbus knew something he had not revealed, that there was some secret precedent that no one else knew about. Oviedo, in his History of the Indies, writes that "some people say" that prior to Columbus' first voyage, a ship loaded with wine and provisions ran into a storm on its way from Spain to England, and was blown far westward. It reportedly arrived in the Indies where "naked people" were seen. Almost everyone died on the long voyage back. Only four or five sailors, who also died soon afterwards, and the pilot survived.

"They also say," continues Oviedo, "that this pilot was a close friend of Christopher Columbus and that he was quite familiar with the route across the high seas to that land which had been found in the manner already mentioned. Very secretly he told Columbus about it who then asked him to make a map and to put the place he had seen on it. They say that Columbus took him into his home as a friend and had him taken care of because the pilot had also fallen ill. But soon afterwards he died, as did his companions. In this way was Columbus informed about this land and the route to it, and the secret remained with him alone."

"As for myself," concludes Oviedo, "I consider this to be untrue." It is an intriguing yarn, but Oviedo's conclusion is probably the correct one.

1483

The King of Portugal
·

*The Portuguese voyages to Africa ✳
Portugal's search for an eastern sea route
to the Orient ✳ Columbus proposes a
westward route to the King, and is rejected*

*João II, King of Portugal from
1481 to 1495. Strongly committed
to geographical exploration, he
sponsored Bartolomeo Diaz'
voyage around the Cape of Good
Hope, but he did not believe in
Columbus' plans.*

Towards the end of his reign, Alfonso V, the Portuguese king who had asked Toscanelli about the route to the Indies, had been forced to dedicate himself more to waging war than to sponsoring voyages of discovery. He had been engaged in conflicts with the Moors, from whom he had taken Tangiers in North Africa in 1470, and with the Castilians. (His wife, Juana la Beltraneya, was the daughter of Henry IV of Castile and a pretender to Queen Isabella's throne.)

Nonetheless, Alfonso did his part to nurture the discoveries begun by Henry the Navigator. In 1469, he granted Fernão Gomes a five-year monoply on trade with Guinea. In return, Gomes was obligated to pay the king an annual fee and to extend Portuguese explorations at least 100 leagues (400 miles, 640 km) further each year from Sierra Leone. Alfonso's son, João II, inherited Gomes' lucrative monopoly at the age of 19. When he rose to the throne in 1481, he thus had a vested interest in helping to encourage further explorations.

But in 1472, Fernando da Poo discovered the island in the Gulf of Guinea that bears his name, and proved that the African coast, after a long bend to the east, turns sharply south instead of continuing towards the Orient. This was a disappointing setback in the search for an eastern sea route to Asia; quite possibly, Alfonso's questions to Toscanelli were related to this development. For this reason, Columbus may have thought that an alternative proposal – westward by sea, instead of eastward – would be met with favor.

The 16th-century Portuguese historian João de Barros writes, "with the notions that had entered his head during many travels and conversations with men who were experts in such matters, and because in Portugal they are very knowledgeable as a result of past discoveries, Christopher Columbus came forward to ask King João for ships to go across this western ocean to discover Cipango."

Columbus also had other good reasons to turn to the

*Below, a 17th-century painting of
Funchal, on the island of Madeira
off the northwest coast of Africa.
The Portuguese arrived there in
1419–20 and immediately began
colonizing it.*

*Above, the River Tagus and
Lisbon, capital city of Portugal.
Columbus saw it for the first time
in 1476, when he was shipwrecked
off Cape St. Vincent. Later he
settled there and married a
Portuguese noblewoman.*

Portuguese king. He had been on Portuguese soil for six or seven years and had married a Portuguese noblewoman. He was part of the Portuguese seafaring world: in *The History of the Indies*, the missionary Bartolomé de Las Casas says that Columbus traveled "in Portuguese company as if he were of their nationality." Finally, he thought of João II as the one *"que entendía en el descubrír más que otro"* –

roughly the same amount that he later asked for in Spain – seemed exorbitant. Moreover, the king and his advisors were already committed to finding an eastward route to Asia by traveling around Africa, and

At right, traffic in the port of Lisbon, from a 16th-century engraving by Theodor de Bry. The planisphere below, from a late-15th-century Latin manuscript, shows Africa in a way that reflects the progress made by Portuguese explorers.

lands. Cão reached the mouth of the Congo River and then the 22nd parallel in present-day Namibia, less than a thousand miles (1,600 km) from the

that is, who, more than any other, understood exploration. In the end, however, João II referred Columbus to a committee, and ultimately rejected his proposal.

João de Barros has some harsh words to say on the matter: he reports that the king was left with the impression that Columbus was a big talker, arrogantly boasting about his own merits, with more fantasies than certainties about "this island of his called Cipango." And Las Casas maintains that King João rejected Columbus' plan because of fears that it would have been impossible to find sailors brave enough to venture out onto the Ocean beyond sight of land. In fact, the king's primary reasons were financial and practical. The funds that Columbus demanded for the undertaking of this voyage –

Columbus' westward route ran contrary to this strategy.

In that same year, if indeed Columbus' interview took place in 1484, João II sent Diego Cão to sea with provisions for three years and a good supply of *padrãos*, stone monuments with the Portuguese coat of arms to mark the newly reached

Caravela - 1460

Portuguese caravels with different rigging, painted on decorative ceramic tiles.

southernmost tip of Africa.

Spurned by King João, Columbus left for Spain with his son Diego, who was about four or five years old. Only he, perhaps, suspected that someday he would return to Portugal in triumph, and that he would prove King João wrong.

Nau redonda - 1498.

A Good Marriage

They met at Mass in a monastery in Lisbon. The marriage probably took place in either the late spring or early fall of 1479. Socially, this was a good marriage for Columbus. His bride, Felipa Moniz Perestrello, was not rich but both her mother's and father's families were noble. Her father was Bartolomeo Perestrello, of the Pallastrelli family from Piacenza in Italy (Perestrello is the Portuguese form of the name); he was a former governor and colonizer of the island of Porto Stefano near Madeira. The young couple settled on Porto Stefano where their son Diego was born. His wife's father, "a great seaman," had died some twenty years before; but according to Fernando Columbus, Perestrello's widow gave Columbus "the documents and navigational charts that her husband had left her: because of these the Admiral's interest was further inflamed and he inquired about the other voyages and sailings that the Portuguese were then taking to La Mina and along the coast of Guinea. And he greatly enjoyed talking with people who had sailed in those parts." It is not known how long his wife Felipa lived. By the time he moved to Castile in 1485, however, Columbus was a widower.

1487
The Wise Men of Salamanca
•
*Columbus proposes a westward route to Queen Isabella and King Ferdinand of Spain * The experts reject his proposal * A Spanish lover and a Spanish son*

In a detail from a popular print, Christopher Columbus defends his geographical ideas before the learned men of Salamanca, while holding up a globe. Its size is similar to that of the oldest known globe, made by Martin Behaim in 1491–1492. Now preserved in Nuremberg, it has a diameter of just over 1.5 feet (50 cm). The commission appointed by the rulers of Castile and Aragon was certainly not prejudiced against Columbus; but from a geographic point of view, given the state of knowledge at the time, there was little credible evidence to support Columbus' theories.

A nd so Columbus once again found himself grappling with a committee. He had traveled to Spain by sea and had landed at the first convenient port, Palos de la Frontera. He may have chosen this harbor because it was near Huelva,

Below, Cathay (China) on a planisphere made in 1459, the work of Fra Mauro.

the home of one of his wife's sisters who would have been able to take care of young Diego. In the monastery of La Rábida, less than four miles (6 km) from the port of Palos, he met Father Antonio de Marchena, a Franciscan who had knowledge of "cosmography and astrology"

– that is, geography and astronomy. At the suggestion of this learned friar, Columbus presented a petition to the royal family of Spain. More precisely, he petitioned both Isabella, Queen of Castile, and Ferdinand, King of Aragon, who jointly ruled their respective separate kingdoms.

At that time, the capital of Spain was wherever the court happened to be; and on January 20, 1486 the court was in Alcalá de Henares,

Columbus in Salamanca. He is slumped wearily on a bench, his gaze lost in the distance, while a monk questions his sanity with a gesture. This detail from a painting by Nicolò Barabino is an effective illustration, but bears little or no reference to historical reality.

where Columbus was granted a royal audience. He had been in Spain for perhaps ten months, the beginning of a frustrating waiting period filled with hopes and burning disappointments that lasted until April 17, 1492. As Oviedo later wrote, "he was for a time in a state of great need and poverty, without being understood by those who heard him."

Columbus presented his project to the Spanish sovereigns and showed them a map, probably drawn by his brother Bartolomeo,

which he would later take with him on his first voyage. There was no immediate verdict; the proposal was referred to a commission of experts, the "wise men of Salamanca." According to popular tradition, these men, who in reality met in either Salamanca or Cordova, foolishly rejected Columbus' inspired plan. The truth is that they listened patiently to a foreigner, albeit a distinguished foreigner from highly respected Genoa, who expounded a project that must have seemed bizarre at the time. Their doubts were well founded: though Columbus' voyage was later seen as a success, the fact remains that he did not reach his proposed goal – Asia – and that his premises were completely wrong according to both 15th-century and modern geography.

Columbus spoke of the splendors of Cathay and

west of the Canaries, whereas Ptolemy put it at 10,000 nautical miles – at least 100 days at sea under the most favorable conditions, and too far to risk the king's money and the lives of his subjects. The commission's negative opinion was communicated to Columbus at a royal audience in a field south of Malaga in August, 1487, while Isabella and Ferdinand

Columbus never married the mother – because, it is said, he did not want a lower-class marriage to stand in his way.

The city of Cordova from a work by Georg Braun (1582–1618). Here, during the difficult years of delays and disappointments, Columbus met the young Beatríz Enríquez de Arana; their son, Fernando, was one of Columbus' first biographers.

The Authority of the Ancients

"On the third day You commanded that the waters gather in the seventh part of the world…." In one of the apocryphal books of the Bible, the fourth book of Esdras, Columbus found this verse to further corroborate his mistaken belief that most of the earth's surface is covered by land rather than water. But he would need still other arguments to convince the "men of Salamanca," and he looked for proofs everywhere in classical texts. At least part of his readings are known. Thanks to his son Fernando, the books annotated in the navigator's handwriting, survive today in the Biblioteca Colombina in Seville. These include a Castilian translation of Plutarch's *Lives*; Landino's Italian translation of Pliny's *Natural History*; a Latin summary of Marco Polo's tale; a historical, geographical miscellany (*Historia rerum ubique gestarum*) filled with references to ancient voyages, and compiled by the humanist Enea Silvio Piccolomini (later Pope Pius II); and the *Imago mundi* by the French theologian Pierre d'Ailly, a cosmographical encyclopedia containing the opinions of ancient geographers. (*Some pages from Columbus' copy of* Imago mundi, *with annotations in his own hand, appear here.*)

Cipango; but his authority was Marco Polo, an author of what today we would call science fiction, not science. He tried to support his theory by citing learned texts; but these "proofs" contradicted the opinion of the acknowledged expert, Ptolemy. And he apparently failed to communicate the force of his own experience, or to convince the committee that he was (as history went on to prove) the kind of man who could sail across the Atlantic seven times without ever going wrong.

In the end, the main point of contention was distance. Columbus argued that Asia lay only 2,400 nautical miles

were at war with the last Islamic kingdom in Spain.

In spite of this verdict, all was not gloomy. In Cordova, where he lived for many months while following the court, Columbus met, perhaps in a pharmacy owned by some countrymen, one Rodrigo de Arana. He was the guardian of his orphaned young cousin, Beatríz, whose family had operated a wine press in the Cordovan mountains. Columbus, who by now was a widower approaching forty, and the twenty-year-old Beatríz became lovers. In August 1488 their son Fernando was born. Though he legitimized their son,

1492

The Spanish Sovereigns

·

*Columbus' years of waiting * Setbacks, and signs of hope * On the field of Santa Fé: success at last * Preparations begin * Difficulties in finding a crew * The three ships are requisitioned*

Columbus did not give up hope after that day in Malaga, but he did look for alternatives. Isabella had paid him 3,000 maravedís, the equivalent of three or four months' pay for an ordinary seaman. She later arranged for him to receive more money on several other occasions. Perhaps that was one reason why Columbus continued to hold on, awaiting the end of the Granada war, which was absorbing the financial resources and energy of the two Spanish kingdoms. Its conclusion seemed close at hand, and Columbus hoped that peace would breathe new life into his proposal. Nonetheless, his brother

Bartolomeo went to Portugal in an effort to renew ties with João II, and then also to England. Christopher himself wrote to the Portuguese sovereign from Seville. He received a polite response

and a safe conduct pass; he may even have taken a trip to Lisbon. Samuel E. Morison, the Columbus scholar, imagines the two brothers on the shores of the Tagus river, watching Bartolomeo Diaz' three ships returning from the Cape of Good Hope in December 1488. It must have been a bitter moment. The Indies were drawing closer, and Columbus was watching the sun set in the Atlantic – from shore.

There were other alternatives: with the support of Father Marchena, Columbus approached two Spanish grandees, Don Enrico Guzmán, the Duke of Medina Sidonia; and then Don Luis de la Cerda, Duke of Medinaceli. While the first nobleman did nothing, the second was won over. According to Bartolomé de Las Casas, Medinaceli was ready to give Columbus "everything that he needed,"

At left, the Franciscan Father Marchena, in a painting by José Roldán in the monastery of La Rábida. He was always a faithful friend to Columbus and generous with his support.

Below, Granada, in an etching from Georg Braun's 16th-century geography book.

including the money to obtain ships, provisions and sailors; first, however, he needed royal approval. But Isabella, again according to Las Casas, was of the opinion that such a venture should only be carried out under the auspices of the Crown; and the Crown, preoccupied with its war with the Moors, did not lift a finger to help.

In the summer of 1489, while Ferdinand was at the siege of Baza, Columbus saw the Queen of Castile at Jaén. There is apparently no truth to the legend that Isabella was willing to pawn her jewels to finance the navigator's expedition, but it *is* certain that she became more favorably disposed towards his project. After the meeting in Jaén, Columbus was sure that he would get what he wanted once the war ended, but the Granada affair seemed endless.

In the autumn of 1491, the man from Genoa went through his hardest time. Discouraged, he headed for the monastery of La Rábida to pick up young Diego, who

GRANATA

A. GRANADA.
B. ALVEISIN.
C. ALHAMBRE.
D. ANTIKVERELA.

was a guest there, with the intention of leaving Spain. At the monastery he met Father Juan Pérez, formerly the queen's confessor. The Franciscan raced to Isabella and persuaded her to summon Columbus back to court. Isabella even sent some money – 20,000 maravedís, which to a sailor represented almost two years' wages.

It must be pointed out that during the long Spanish period Columbus was able to count on devoted friends,

Above, Ferdinand of Aragon and Isabella of Castile, the rulers who laid the foundation of a unified Spain, from a relief in the Capilla Real in Granada.

without whom he could not have survived. A group of supporters had formed at court (perhaps some enrolled after his success!). Those who helped him, in addition to Fathers Marchena and Pérez, were the Duke of Medinaceli; the powerful Spanish primate, Cardinal Mendoza; Father Diego Deza, a theologian in Salamanca who later became Archbishop of Seville; Doña Juana de Torres, the royal governess; the court treasurer Alonso de Quintanilla; even, it seems, Father Fernando de Talavera, president of the commission of experts that had left Columbus in limbo.

At left, Father Diego Deza, painted by Francisco Zurbarán. A theologian who later became Archbishop of Seville, Deza took Columbus under his wing during the years of waiting in Spain.

Granada finally surrendered on January 2, 1492. Immediately the queen agreed to reopen the discussion of Columbus' proposal – the great voyage, discovery, glory and riches promised to Spain. On the field in Santa Fé, waiting to witness the sovereigns' entry into Granada, were gathered all the decision-makers: three archbishops, fourteen bishops, the Grand Masters of the orders of Santiago and Alcantara, dukes, marquises, counts, even scholars. It seems that they had decided to rule favorably on the scientific evidence, perhaps to please the queen; but as before in Portugal, the royal council was frightened by Columbus' price. As payment, he demanded the perpetual rank of Admiral of the Ocean, equal to that of the Grand Admiral of Castile; appointment as Governor

and Viceroy of all the lands that would be discovered; the right to ten percent of the subsequent trade revenues; and hereditary rights to the titles and privileges granted.

As a result of these demands, "the deal completely went up in smoke," according to his son. Columbus got on his mule and took the road to Seville. He intended to embark for France. He had only traveled four miles (6 km) when a messenger caught up with him and called him back. On April 17, 1492, the sovereigns ratified the "capitulations" – that is, the contract – and agreed to all the conditions demanded by the stubborn man from Genoa.

Below, despite what this lovely tapestry shows, Queen Isabella never sold or pawned her jewels to finance Columbus' expedition.

How Much Did It Cost to Discover America?

It is estimated that Columbus' first voyage cost two million maravedís. Of this amount, 360,000 maravedís were "contributed" by the city of Palos. Columbus himself raised another 500,000 maravedís from his Genoese banker friends. The remaining amount was secured by Santángel again through loans.

In 1942, Samuel Eliot Morison tried to convert the cost of Columbus' first voyage – two million maravedís – into U.S. currency, and arrived at a figure of $14,000. Another comparison: a few years after the voyage, the "poorest" of Spain's 13 dukes had an annual income that was about five times greater than all the funds raised for Columbus' voyage. These comparisons suggest that Columbus' expedition was, in modern terms, a relatively low-budget operation.

The church of St. George in Palos was built on the remains of an early Christian place of worship. On May 23, 1492 the local people were ordered to assemble in this twenty-year-old church, and a notary read aloud the royal document ordering them to furnish two ships to Captain-General Christopher Columbus. In attendance were the local authorities, Columbus, and his friend Father Pérez, a Franciscan from the monastery of La Rábida. The event is recorded in this painting by Bejarano in this same monastery of La Rábida which has today become a site devoted to Columbus memorabilia. The monastery rises on a hill about four miles (6 km) outside the little city of Palos.

Shortly after Columbus mounted his mule to leave the field of Santa Fé, whether out of despair, anger, or with the cool daring of a gambler who raises the stakes when he feels he has a good hand, the tide turned suddenly in his favor. Isabella and Ferdinand abruptly decided to accept his demands. The man instrumental in changing their minds was Luis de Santángel, *escribano de ración* – that is, royal treasurer.

Santángel was a lay brother who had business relationships with members of Spain's Genoese community, including some to whom the Court was substantially indebted. He looked at Columbus' proposal from a practical point of view. Columbus'

belief in a westward route to the Indies was unsupported by hard evidence, but the "scientific" arguments which denied its possibility were themselves doubtful. Columbus' demands were exorbitant, but nothing would be owed to him if there were no results. The amount of money immediately needed for the expedition was small and could be found easily: because of certain infractions, a fine could be imposed on the city of Palos, requiring the town to furnish two fully equipped ships. Santángel himself would know how to provide the rest.

Isabella and Ferdinand, persuaded by these arguments, ordered preparations to be made for

the great voyage. After ten long years of frustration and waiting, things began to move swiftly for Columbus. Now time was being measured in weeks, in days. Before autumn was past, the expedition would be organized and on its way.

Palos, a port on the Tinto River open to the Atlantic, was chosen as the port of departure – perhaps because of the "infractions" noted by Santángel, or because the boatwrights there knew how to build caravels like the ones used so successfully by Portuguese explorers. On May 23, 1492 in the church of St. George in Palos, the notary read the sovereigns' order in public. Columbus was appointed commander of a fleet of three ships whose destination was left vague: *ciertas partes de la mar Oceana* ("certain parts of the Ocean"). A pardon was promised to convicts who enlisted, but only four actually signed up. Legend has it that Columbus' crew was made up of criminals, but this is a demonstrably false story that defames the many good and brave sailors who joined the perilous voyage.

It is true, however, that the seamen of Palos, Moguer, and Huelva did not rush to enlist in spite of the Queen of Castile's decree, and that the local population was sceptical of the Admiral's grand plan. Many years later, in testimony gathered for the lawsuit pitting Columbus' heirs against the Crown, the evidence of a man from Moguer clearly states that "many people made fun of" Columbus. "They mocked him" and "ridiculed him in public" for dreaming to "discover the Indies."

The crew shortage was finally remedied when Columbus, thanks once more to the patronage of Father Marchena, met Martín Alonso Pinzón, an experienced captain who had

Of the expedition's three ships, one was chartered by Columbus and the other two were furnished by the city of Palos as commanded by royal decree. The preparations went very quickly. In the engraving above, a sailing ship from a later time is being loaded. In the summer of 1492, the atmosphere was no different.

The *Niña*'s owner, Juan Niño, was her first mate.

Columbus quickly found the third ship, a Galician vessel that was rechristened the *Santa Maria* and was designated as the Admiral's flagship. Her owner, Juan de la Cosa, whom Columbus had met when he was dealing with the Duke of Medinaceli, signed on as first mate. The pilot was Pero Alonso Niño. The commissary – *alguacil*

Another painting, below, records the meeting between Columbus and the Pinzón brothers. Pictured here are, from left, Father Marchena with his hand on the shoulder of young Diego, the eldest of Columbus' sons; Father Pérez; Columbus himself, standing; and seated at the table, the Pinzóns.

just returned from carrying barrels of sardines to the mouth of the Tiber River. Thanks to Pinzón's influence, which was great in that region, Columbus was able to sign on the remaining crew members.

Columbus was impressed with Martín Alonso Pinzón, and put him in command of the *Pinta*, one of the two ships contributed to the expedition by the city of Palos. His younger brother Francisco was made first mate of the *Pinta* and another brother, Vicente Yañez Pinzón, was given command of the second ship, the *Niña*.

mayor de la armada – was Diego de Arana, the cousin of Columbus' mistress Beatríz. Luis de Torres was made the official interpreter because he knew three languages – Hebrew, Chaldaic, and a little Arabic – and it was thought these would enable him to talk to the inhabitants of Japan and China when they arrived in Asia. Pedro Sánchez had the job of weighing the gold, and of

setting aside the Crown's share.

In all there were some 90 men, 87 of whose names we know. Other than a ship's boy from Genoa and another from Portugal, two Italian sailors, and the Admiral himself, all the crew members were Spaniards. One was from Murcia, ten were from northern Spain (Galicians and Basques), and the others were southerners from Andalusia.

At left, the "brain trust" of Columbus' first voyage. On the far left is Juan de la Cosa, owner of the flagship Santa Maria *and the Captain General's second in command. In the center is Vicente Yañez Pinzón, captain of the* Niña. *At right is Martín Alonso Pinzón, captain of the* Pinta. *Another of the Pinzón brothers, Francisco Martín, was second in command on the* Pinta.

The Niña, Pinta, and Santa Maria

•

What did Columbus' ships look like? ∗ Caravels and Carracks, Lateen and Square Rigs ∗ Navigation using a compass, quadrant, and sandglass ∗ Difficulties in calculating time, distance, and position

Above, a reconstruction of the Pinta, the larger of the two caravels. Since both the mainsail and the foresail were square-rigged, it was called a round caravel (redonda). Columbus considered it to be la mas velera, the fastest of his three ships.

Below, another reconstruction of the Santa Maria. The original Santa Maria crossed the Atlantic with some 40 people on board, 39 of whose names we know. It must have been uncomfortably crowded, since it was less than 79 feet (24m) long.

The type of ship preferred by 15th-century explorers was the caravel, which had been invented, or perfected, by the Portuguese for sailing along the African coast. It was easy to maneuver, fast, and usually lateen-rigged, which enabled it to sail closer to the wind than traditional square-rigged ships. We can assume that Columbus, like most sailors of that period, had a high opinion of these vessels.

Below, a Spanish reconstruction of the Santa Maria, showing some of her interior.

But of the three ships that Columbus assembled in Palos, only two were caravels, of which one was square-rigged and the other (at least at the outset) was lateen.

What did the ships look like? One tantalizing clue is provided by Pietro Martire d'Anghiera, whose *New World* (1511) provides a description of Columbus' ships that has been a source of debate among naval archaeologists. Here is the original Latin passage: "*Tria nauigia: unum onerarium caveatum. Alia duo mercatoria*

Above, the Niña is reconstructed here with three masts, all of them lateen-rigged.

levia sine caveis, quae ab hispanis caravelae vocantur." Earlier scholars thought that *caveatum* meant "with a deck," which would mean that the Santa Maria had an upper deck and the other two ships did not. Today it is believed that *caveatum* refers to a top, a kind of platform around a mast to which rigging was attached. If this is correct, Pietro Martire was describing "three vessels, one a cargo ship with a top, the other two light merchantmen without tops, of the type the Spanish call caravels." The "cargo ship" refers to the Santa Maria. Columbus called it a *nao* – that is, simply a "ship" – but it was probably what was known as a carrack, a general term for any large merchant ship or galleon.

Our knowledge of Columbus' ships is largely based on educated guesswork, as no definitive records exist. Martinez Hidalgo, Director of the Maritime Museum in Barcelona, believes that the Santa Maria was almost three times as long as it was wide, and that the two caravels were slightly more elongated in shape. He also believes that the three ships had a "height" – i.e., a vertical

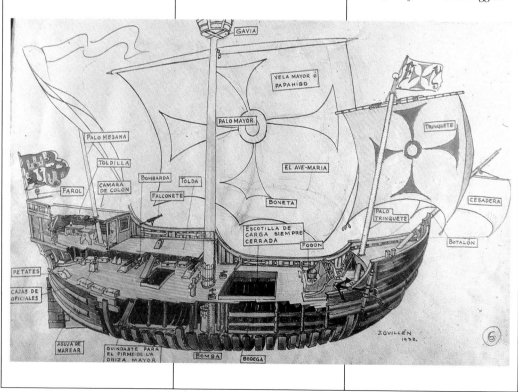

Above, a pontoon has come alongside a newly launched ship. The masts and rudder have not yet been rigged; the ballast is also missing, judging by how high she rides in the water. The top-heavy ships of this time required a great deal of ballast; the Santa Maria, *for example, must have carried about 20 tons (over 18,000 kg) of ballast.*

distance above and below the waterline – that was about six or seven times greater than the width. In other words, compared to modern vessels these vessels were broad and very top-heavy. What is truly astonishing, however, is how small these ships were. The length of the hulls ranged from little more than 77 feet (23.5m) for the *Santa Maria*, to about 70.5 feet (21.5m) for the *Niña*.

Both the *Santa Maria* and the *Pinta* had three masts plus a bowsprit. The foremast was near the bow of the ship, the mainmast was towards the middle, the mizzenmast was near the stern, and the bowsprit was an almost horizontal spar jutting forward from the bow. The

first two masts each had a square sail, with the mainsail being the largest. The mainmast on the *Santa Maria* must have been over 85 feet high (26m), and the yard that supported the mainsail was about 52 feet (16m). Both ships could unfurl a square sail – the spiritsail – beneath the bowsprit, but only the *Santa Maria* had a top sail rigged above the mainsail. The third or mizzenmast on both ships had a lateen sail, which was very useful for maneuvering.

The legendary *Niña*, the caravel that Columbus preferred and on which he sailed at least 25,000 miles (40,000 km), was originally lateen-rigged. This means it had triangular sails rigged almost parallel to the length of the hull. When they were unfurled, each sail looked like a sideways "V" with the tip pointing down and forward towards the bow, and the broad end stretching up. It is not certain whether the *Niña* had two masts or three, but almost surely the masts and sails decreased in

Below, a late-15th-century merchant ship, from an Italian manuscript of the time. Ships of this period had remarkably wide mainsails. According to recent reconstructions, the main yard of the Santa Maria *was at least 52 feet (16m) long, twice the width of the hull.*

size from the bow to the stern. Later, after arriving in the Canary Islands and before crossing the unfamiliar ocean, Columbus had the *Niña*'s rigging changed from lateen to square, after which she probably resembled the *Pinta*, but without the spiritsail.

The real difference between the caravels and the *Santa Maria* lay in their nautical properties. The caravels were much better at sailing into the wind, which made them more maneuverable and more adaptable to different wind conditions. The caravels were also faster than the *Santa Maria*. This irritated Martín Alonso Pinzón, captain of the *Pinta*, who was often forced to take in sail so as not to leave Columbus' flagship behind.

These, then, were the small and fragile ships being readied in the port of Palos during the summer of 1492. The crewmen, wearing red caps to distinguish them from farmers or common laborers, busied themselves with last-minute preparations under Columbus' impatient eye. He apparently had no doubts about the seaworthiness of his vessels. A modern sailor would consider them mere twigs in the ocean, but Columbus was confident they were equal to the task.

Navigational instruments: at left, the sandglass as it was in the 15th and 16th centuries; below, two examples of a sun clock – that is, a kind of portable sundial – from the end of the 16th century. To measure time, Columbus had only the sandglass which was periodically synchronized with the sun.

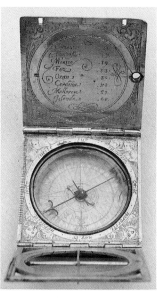

Above, an astrolabe. The astrolabe was a refined astronomical instrument used to measure the elevation of a star in degrees. However, its use at sea was often impractical; most navigators used a quadrant instead. By Columbus' time, the compass had undergone two fundamental improvements. First, the magnetic needle was placed on a fixed pivot instead of floating on water; second, the needle was affixed to a "wind rose" or compass card that rotated with the needle. The horizon was not divided into degrees, but rather into 32 points.

Every eight turns of the sandglass – that is, every four hours – the old watch was replaced and fresh crewmen took their place. The helmsman, whose four hours at the helm were now up, gave the compass course to the officer in command of the new watch. The officer repeated the course to the new helmsman who in turn repeated it aloud. This was a precaution to avoid misunderstandings. To a tired sailor, for example, an order to steer "sudueste cuarta al sur" (southwest by south) might be mistaken for "sur cuarta al sudueste" (south by west); in this case, the mistake would result in a 22.5° error, taking the vessel far off course.

After confirming the course, the helmsman began his work. He in no way resembled the helmsman portrayed in Hollywood epics, grasping the wheel, bravely facing the storm-driven waves sweeping across the deck. Most people do not realize that in Columbus' day the helmsman was below deck and could see neither the sea ahead nor the sails. Moreover, the ship's wheel was an early-18th-century innovation; Columbus' helmsmen used a tiller, a handle connected directly to the rudder. The stern rudder was one of the most important nautical improvements made in the Middle Ages. It replaced both the two side rudders used by the Romans and other Mediterranean sailors, and the starboard side-rudder used on Viking ships. The steering mechanism on Columbus' ships was hinged to the right side of the stern, and the tiller that moved it came into a lower deck – the "quarterdeck" – where the helmsman stood. On the Santa Maria, *the quarterdeck was where the officers slept and stowed their gear. The helmsman steered the ship, following the officer of the watch's instructions which were communicated to him through a hatch.*

In theory, at least, navigation is very simple. First, you must set a course in a particular direction and follow it with the help of a compass. Second, from time to time you must check your position (this is known as taking a "ship's fix"). Using traditional means, a "ship's fix" requires a sextant, a chronometer or clock, and an "ephemerides" or table listing the position of the stars and

planets at given times.

But of all these instruments, only one – the magnetic compass – existed in Columbus' day. His compass was a relatively primitive instrument. It was equipped with gimbals to lessen the effects of the ship's motion. It had a magnetic needle and a so-called "wind rose" or compass card that showed the four cardinal directions (north, east, south, west) and the intermediate directions halfway between the cardinal points (northeast, southeast, southwest, and northwest). These eight basic directions were further divided into four "points" corresponding to slightly more than 11°. In short, the horizon was divided into 32 points instead of 360°, which means that directions were measured roughly rather than precisely. The accuracy was further decreased by the fact that no account was taken either of "declination"

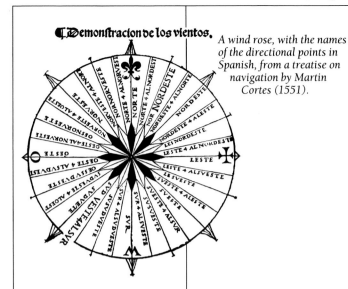

Demonftracion de los vientos.

A wind rose, with the names of the directional points in Spanish, from a treatise on navigation by Martin Cortes (1551).

Speed was a matter of guesswork: instruments like the log line did not yet exist, so speed was estimated by looking at the flow of water along the hull. Time was measured with a sandglass which was turned every half hour. The rate at which the sand flowed could be affected by the ship's movement, and because the hour of midday became progressively later as the ships sailed westward, it was necessary periodically to

an experienced sailor could compensate for the lack of reliable instruments, but only up to a point. When land was sighted from the *Niña* on the first return voyage in 1493, some on board thought that it was Madeira. Others believed it was the Portuguese coast. Columbus was a more skillful navigator, and correctly thought that the landfall was one of the Azores. But even he did not know which island in this

(the difference between geographical north and magnetic north, which varies from place to place) or of "deviation" (the shifting of the needle caused by nearby metal objects).

It was virtually impossible to use celestial navigation for the measurement of longitude – that is, east-to-west distance – because there were no chronometers. To find latitude – that is, north-to-south location – the height of the sun at its meridian (noon) was measured, or in the northern hemisphere the height of the North Star. Sailors used an instrument called a quadrant for making these measurements; but the quadrant was so difficult to use on a rolling ship that reliable measurements could be made only through repeated land-based observations. Under the

proper conditions, however, the quadrant could be fairly exact. In 1503–1504, for instance, Columbus calculated – on land – the latitude of Saint Gloria Bay in Jamaica with an error of less than one-half a degree. By the standards of his day, this was a bull's-eye.

Given the primitive state of navigational instruments, the "ship's fix" in Columbus' day was usually only a rough approximation. It was necessary to know or to estimate three elements: time, speed, direction. Based on these, the route taken from the point of departure could be marked on the chart. Direction was given by the compass. It was relatively easy to record successive changes in the course, but much more difficult to calculate the effects of drift or of the movement of currents.

De las agujas

At right, a wind rose depicted in a navigational treatise by Pedro Medina (1552).

Notable quarto de las agujas de na-uegar.

synchronize the sandglass with the sun. Columbus did this on a weekly basis, using a method that probably was accurate within a quarter of an hour.

The skill and knowledge of

350-mile-long (560 km) chain had been sighted: such was the state of navigational science in his day.

Details from 16th-century allegorical engravings about the voyages of discovery. At left, the captain, at sea, has a quadrant in his hand (but is not using it). At right, he is making observations with an armillary sphere (a ringed model of the heavens). At the time, only repeated measurements made on land were reliable.

Life at Sea

·

*A sailor's day * The watch * Food and drink aboard a 15th-century ship * The crew's faith in their captain*

Time was marked by the sandglass which the ship's boy turned every half hour, and by the changing of the watch every four hours. (The first watch came on at 3:00 a.m., the next at 7:00 a.m., and so forth.) The crew was divided into two squads, or watches, which took turns working under a rotating command of officers (either the captain, the pilot, the master or the boatswain). When it was time for the new watch to come on, it was literally called to duty: bells were not yet used to regulate life at sea.

The day began with the scrubbing of the deck with sea water and brooms, followed by the morning prayer. It ended when the galley fire was put out and with more prayers. (The *Pater Noster*, *Ave Maria*, and *Credo* were recited and the *Salve Regina* was sung.) The difficulty of the work depended largely on the weather and on how many maneuvers were needed to keep the ship on course. In any case, there were always the typical seaman's chores to do, maintaining and repairing sails and lines. The bilge pump was started every day by the morning watch. A storm or any other emergency would bring all hands on deck.

When the sun was up, someone woke the captain, bringing him a bucket of water to wash with. He was the only one with his own cabin. Everyone else slept where he could. Hammocks were unknown – they were discovered later in America – and sleeping conditions must have been extremely crowded and uncomfortable.

Hot food was cooked on a *fogón* or stove, which on the *Santa Maria* was located on deck immediately behind the forecastle. One hot meal was served every day, at noon, and then only if conditions

Above, this detail from a painting by Cornelis Anthonjszoon shows "sailors aloft" trimming the sails of a Portuguese carrack; some are on the topsail yard, others are in the caveatum, *a platform to which rigging was attached.*

permitted: in bad weather, it was impossible to keep the fire lit. Water and wine – Spanish sailors expected and received much of the latter – were kept in wooden casks which were inspected

MARINA DEL RENACIMIENTO
CARABELAS DEL SIGLO XVI.

At left, a Spanish caravel at sea, from a painting in the Madrid Naval Museum. The rigging is set and the watch on duty does not have much to do at the moment. On the poop deck, the officer of the watch. The helmsman can not be seen; his station is below deck.

• LVNA •

L a luna al nauigar molto conforta
Er in peschare et ucellare et caccia
Amu i suoi figlinoli aprc la porta
Et anche al solazzare che ao altri piaccia :·

At left, ships and sailors in a detail from a 15th-century manuscript. According to a universally held opinion, a sailor's life in late medieval Europe was hard and dangerous – although maybe no more so, according to one famous naval historian, than the life of a typical 19th-century industrial worker. Certainly it was an uncomfortable life. In the naval architecture of the time, for example, no provision was made for any area that could be called crew's quarters. The sailors had few personal belongings: a Genoese document dated 1493 includes an inventory of a sailor's trunk, the contents of which consisted of two overcoats and a cloth tunic, two shirts, one pair of cloth underwear, three pairs of footwear and four handkerchiefs.

not suffer from scurvy or other diseases associated with this unappetizing and unhealthy diet.

As for wages, we have this record from Columbus' fourth voyage: seamen earned 1000 maravedís a month, ship's boys 800 maravedís, and the ship's captain four times as much as a seaman.

Like all "who go down to the sea in ships, to trade on the high seas" (Psalm 106), Columbus' crew placed their trust in God, in the quality of their ship, in their own professional abilities, and above all in the skill of their captain. And according to Michele da Cuneo, a friend of Columbus, their captain's skill was unsurpassed: "From the time that Genoa was Genoa, there never was born a more magnanimous man or one more penetrating in matters of navigation than the aforementioned Admiral; so that when sailing, on just seeing a cloud or a star by night, he could judge what would come next; and if there was to be bad weather, he himself would take command and stay at the helm; and after the storm passed, he hoisted the sails and the others slept."

In this painting by Daniel Vasques, which hangs today in the monastery of La Rábida in Palos, Columbus is pictured wearing the simple clothing typical of a sailor of that time, a short gray wool tunic belted at the waist.

frequently to make sure they were still intact and did not roll around in the hold. The other food supplies were primarily hardtack (a kind of biscuit), salted meat and fish, and olive oil. Columbus also mentions cheese, lentils, beans, honey, rice, almonds, and raisins in his list of provisions for later Atlantic crossings. He recommends having fishing tackle on board; fresh fish must have been a welcome variation in the diet. The amount of food was sufficient, but its nutritional value was low. Fortunately, Columbus' crossing was a quick one and his crew did

On the late medieval ship, at right, the crow's-nest, a railed-in platform at the top of the mast, is clearly visible. From this vantage point, a lookout scanned the horizon with his naked eye; the spyglass did not come into use until later.

1492
The Voyage of Discovery Begins

•

*The three ships set sail from Palos, and head for the Canary Islands * Columbus leaves the Canary Islands behind * Slow going in the Sargasso Sea, then fresh winds, and – at last! – land.*

In the early hours of Friday, August 3, 1492, Christopher Columbus gathered his captains, pilots and crew in the church of St. George in Palos. They heard Mass, confessed their sins, received communion and then embarked. In the harbor, on the left bank of the Tinto River, the three ships slipped their moorings and glided slowly downstream on the ebb tide, sails empty, as people on shore waved farewell in the long shadows of dawn.

At the bar of Saltes, the sandbank between the mouth of the river and the ocean, a light breeze began to swell the heavy canvas sails. The soft creaking of straining timbers and hemp lines could be heard. At sunset, land was still in sight, but the north wind began to blow. During the night the helmsmen finally set the course: *suroeste cuarta al sur*, southwest by south (about 214°), the route to the Canary Islands.

Why the Canaries? True, that chain of islands was the westernmost Spanish territory and a good place to take on supplies of water, wood, and meat before beginning the unknown part of the trip; and it is equally true that on Gomera, one of the islands, the acting governor was a woman whom Columbus loved. (It is not certain, however, if he knew her at this time). The choice of this port of call must in reality be thought of as a part of an ingenious nautical strategy. The 16th-century historian Francesco Guicciardini wrote in his *History of Italy* that Columbus "having many times sailed the Ocean sea, and surmising, based on his observation of certain winds, that which then truly happened to him, he sailed to the west and discovered … some islands about which before there had been no knowledge." The key lies in the words "observation of certain winds." During the years in which he traveled the Atlantic, Columbus had at least guessed the existence

At right, Columbus' departure, with ships propelled by oars and the Spanish sovereigns waving from the shore, as it was imagined in an engraving published in 1621. Below, the Captain General takes leave of Ferdinand and Isabella before going down to the port to embark. Like many "historical" recreations of this moment, it is without factual basis: Theodor de Bry made this picture many years after the event.

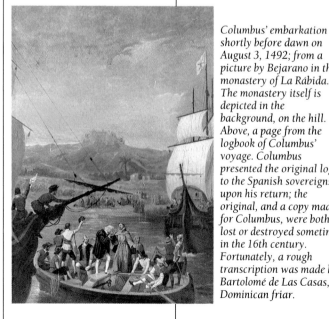

Columbus' embarkation shortly before dawn on August 3, 1492; from a picture by Bejarano in the monastery of La Rábida. The monastery itself is depicted in the background, on the hill. Above, a page from the logbook of Columbus' voyage. Columbus presented the original log to the Spanish sovereigns upon his return; the original, and a copy made for Columbus, were both lost or destroyed sometime in the 16th century. Fortunately, a rough transcription was made by Bartolomé de Las Casas, a Dominican friar.

of steady trade winds. Heading to the Canaries and then following the 28th northern parallel, he entered and kept himself within the limit of the favorable trade wind from the northeast.

The route to the Canaries took Columbus through familiar waters, but still there was no lack of trouble. On August 6, the *Pinta* already had a damaged rudder; Columbus, rather improbably, suspected sabotage. Then, while heading to Las Palmas on Grand Canary for repairs, she had to remain for two weeks within sight of the island before being able to come into port. In the meantime, Columbus had sailed to Gomera and back, and ordered the *Niña*'s lateen sails to be replaced with square

Above, a view of the Canary Islands, about 250 miles (400 km) off the west coast of Morocco,

Columbus' last sight of land before setting off towards the New World.

rigging. Finally, on September 2, the three ships rocked in Gomera's San Sebastián Bay. A month had already passed, when ordinarily it took only eight or ten days at sea to reach this point.

Columbus weighed anchor again on September 6. The weather was dead calm and his ships bobbed in the Atlantic swells. Finally, at 3:00 a.m. on September 9, the trade winds began to blow. By sunset, they were out of sight of land: the island of Hierro, the westernmost of the Canaries, and the Pico de Teide, the volcanic peak on Tenerife, had finally

Above, a fresco in Genoa shows Columbus' ships proceeding down the Tinto River on their way to the Atlantic Ocean.

Below, the African coast and the Canary Islands naively portrayed in a Venetian book dating from 1528.

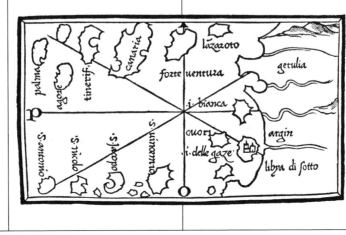

A Love Affair in the Canaries

There was a castle overlooking the beach in San Sebastián where Columbus' ships finished taking on provisions. It was the home of Beatríz de Peraza y Bobadilla, the widow of Gomera's governor. (Her husband Hernán Peraza had been killed by the Canary Islanders, who resented his overbearing and cruel rule.) Columbus apparently loved her. Michele da Cuneo, a nobleman from Savona and a friend of the Columbus family, uses the picturesque expression "tinged with love" to describe the Admiral's feelings, but that is all that is known for sure about this romance. Doña Beatríz had lived on Gomera since 1482. At the age of 17, this beautiful noblewoman became first the queen's maid of honor and then the king's lover. As a punishment, Isabella forced her to marry Peraza. Presumably, this was also Isabella's way of punishing Peraza, one of whose vassals had recently murdered a Spanish nobleman. Doña Beatríz was widowed after six years, but when Columbus stopped at Gomera she was still young, beautiful, and impulsive. The details of her relationship with Columbus are unknown; what is known is that Columbus and his fleet passed by Gomera again in 1493, and that Doña Beatríz greeted him with artillery salvos, public illuminations, and fireworks. By the time of Columbus' third voyage, in 1498, their passion (if it ever existed) was dead: Doña Beatríz had become the lover of the future ruler of the Grand Canary Island, whom she later married. Later she was apparently killed, either for reasons of State or for revenge: after she hanged two people – one accused her of immorality, the other was a political enemy – the Spanish sovereigns summoned her back to court to explain her actions. A few days later she was found dead.

A watercolor by Rafael Monleon showing the Santa Maria and the Pinta under sail. Helped by the trade winds, the crossing was smooth and relatively swift – but not swift enough for the crews, who may have become mutinous towards the end of the voyage.

MARINA DE LA EDAD MEDIA.
SIGLO XVI.
CARABELAS DE COLON.

disappeared over the horizon. Right away, Columbus decided to keep a double record of the distance traveled. He privately recorded the actual distance which he thought had been traveled each day; in the official log, however, he deliberately understated the distance by jotting down a smaller number. He probably did this to avoid raising the crew's expectations too soon: if the Indies turned out to be further away than the Admiral calculated, his men would be none the wiser and less likely to grumble.

The winds were steady, the sea calm, and the air mild. On September 16, Columbus wrote in his logbook that "it was like April in Andalusia. The mornings were truly enjoyable. The only thing missing was the nightingale's song." On this same day, the ships entered the Sargasso Sea, a part of the Gulf Stream filled, as Columbus noted, with "a great quantity of very green seaweed." He mistakenly speculated that this seaweed "had not very long before broken off from the land."

There was evidence that the compass was deviating

Big World, Big Mistake

On September 23, the Pinta's crew thought (incorrectly) that they had sighted land. By then, according to Columbus' estimates, his ships had traveled 2,400 nautical miles (4400 km) and therefore should be approaching the coast of "Cipango" or Japan. Columbus believed this because he had greatly underestimated the size of the earth. He thought that each degree of longitude measured 45 nautical miles, and that therefore the earth's circumference was only 16,200 nautical miles (30,000 km). In fact, one degree of longitude equals 60 nautical miles, and the earth's actual circumference is 21,600 nautical miles (40,000 km). In short, Columbus underestimated the earth's size by 25 per cent. This error, combined with his belief that the earth's land masses were much larger and the oceans were much smaller than is actually the case, led him to think that he had almost reached the shores of Asia. He was, of course, greatly mistaken.

from magnetic north, but Columbus provided an explanation aimed at keeping the crew calm: "It seems that it is the polar star which is changing its position, not the compass needle." The unchanging direction of the wind also worried his men, since it would hinder their return. Columbus had already concluded that on his return voyage he would have to follow a more northerly route, in the west wind zone, but he considered himself lucky when on September 22 his men experienced a day of contrary winds. There were also false sightings of land: clouds on the horizon were often mistaken for the shores they awaited with ever-growing impatience.

With the arrival of October, the trade winds began to pick up. Morison has calculated that for five consecutive days the ships made an average of 142 nautical miles (263 km) and, on October 7, the Niña announced another sighting of land and flocks of birds flew in the sky towards the west-southwest. Columbus changed course to follow

Below left, the Admiral studies the itineraries of his explorations. From a painting kept in Seville. Below, the route of the first Atlantic crossing, with the ship's day-to-day progress, reconstructed from the data in Columbus' logbook.

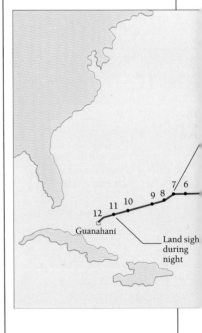

Guanahaní

Land sigh during night

The constellation Ursa Minor ("the Little Bear") was used by sailors as a sort of luminous nighttime clock. At the center of this clock is Polaris, the North Star. A gigantic watch hand is formed by drawing an imaginary line between the North Star and Kocab, another bright star in the same constellation. As the earth turns, the North Star appears to remain stationary while Kocab – the tip of the hand – slowly circles it just like the hour hand of a real clock. In Columbus' day there were charts, with a human figure in a circle and the North Star in the center, to make this observation easier.

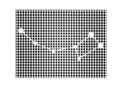

them. (The change caused him to miss Florida, but took him on the shortest route to the nearest land.) Perhaps mutiny was in the air. On October 9, according to Oviedo, Columbus promised to turn back if land was not sighted within three days. Meanwhile, they continued to race along in the ever-stronger trade wind, with speeds up to 9 knots on October 11.

On October 12, at 2 o'clock in the morning, the lookout on the *Pinta*, Juan Rodríguez Bermejo, sighted land by moonlight. Taking in sail, the squadron tacked until morning, then rounded a point and found a landing on the leeward side. They had reached Watling Island – Guanahaní to the inhabitants, and San Salvador as Columbus christened it – one of the Bahamas, which the natives called Lucaye. Columbus himself had seen a

The high point in Columbus' life was undoubtedly the moment when he first set foot in the New World. He christened this landfall San Salvador; modern historians believe that it corresponds to present-day Watling Island in the Bahamas. Here the scene is imagined by 19th-century painter Giovanni Battista Carlone.

light at sea the previous night at 10 o'clock. It has often been thought that the Genoese Admiral made this claim in order to seize credit for the sighting, and to secure for himself the annual pension promised to the first man who sighted land. But some historians believe Columbus' claim: Ruth Wolper points out that from where the *Santa Maria* lay at that time, a bonfire – lit, perhaps, to keep insects away from the huts – on the windward cliff of Watling would have been visible.

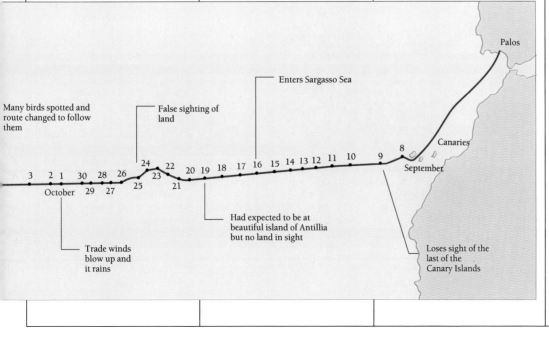

Many birds spotted and route changed to follow them

False sighting of land

Enters Sargasso Sea

Palos

Canaries

September

Had expected to be at beautiful island of Antillia but no land in sight

Trade winds blow up and it rains

Loses sight of the last of the Canary Islands

3 2 1 30 28 26 24 22 20 19 18 17 16 15 14 13 12 11 10 9 8
October 29 27 25 23 21

The New Era Begins

•

*Columbus sets foot in the New World * His first encounter with the Caribbean natives * The discovery of Cuba * The search for gold and the Great Khan*

Columbus' logbook gives us a vivid impression of those historic first moments. Even before disembarking, Columbus and his men see "naked people" and around the white sand beach "very green trees, many waters and fruits of different kinds." Columbus goes ashore with the royal standard. With him are the captains, the two Pinzón brothers, carrying banners marked with the letters F (for King Ferdinand) and Y (for Queen "Ysabella") surmounted by a crown on either side of a cross. Rodrígo de Escobedo draws up a proclamation claiming possession of the island for Spain. It is a solemn moment. In the shade of the trees, the people who live on the island watch and then, curious, draw nearer.

The native Americans who witnessed Columbus' landing were called the Tainos. They belonged to the Arawakan language group; in the previous century, they had spread out from Haiti and occupied the Bahamas as well as most of Cuba, Jamaica, and Puerto Rico, displacing more primitive tribes. Theirs was an agricultural society. They cultivated maize (Indian corn), sweet potatoes and other vegetables. They wove cotton and made terracotta pots. They played with rubber balls and danced

Above, right, an imaginative recreation of Columbus' first encounter with native Americans, with sword in hand and the jingling of little bells.

Below, a 16th-century portrait of an "Indian." The Caribbean natives looked very different from the African, Oriental, and Caucasian races with which Europeans were familiar; in spite of this clue, it did not occur to Columbus that he had discovered a New World rather than Asia.

to the sound of wooden drums. They treated Columbus with hospitality and kindness.

In his log during the first two days ashore, Columbus wrote that "they go about naked as their mother bore them, even the women. I never saw anyone of them who was over thirty years

old. They are very well-proportioned, with very beautiful bodies and very pretty faces. They all have very broad foreheads" and "very large, beautiful eyes." Columbus then notes that "they must be good servants and of quick intelligence, because I see that they very quickly learn everything I tell them and I believe that they can easily become Christians, since it seems that they have no religion." (This was incorrect. The Tainos venerated the Moon and Sun.)

Below, sailing in the islands. This woodcut appeared in an illustrated edition of the letter Columbus sent to Gabriel Sanchez in 1493, immediately after his return from the New World. The letter was dispatched from Lisbon, and was intended to serve as an "official report" for the benefit of Isabella and Ferdinand.

The elaborate ornaments pictured in this 16th-century print suggests that American tribal societies had a rich cultural tradition. But such pictures were conditioned by European conventions, and can only hint at what these vanished societies were really like.

he named Santa Maria de la Concepción (now called Rum Cay), Fernandina (Long Island), and Isabella (Crooked Island). He was impressed with the natural splendors of this new world.

At right, cooking fish; an illustration by Theodor de Bry. Oviedo says in his History of the Indies *that "the Indians' most common food, and the one they are most fond of, is fish from the rivers and the sea; and the Indians are very clever and skilled in the art of catching them."*

On Fernandina, he wrote, "there are vast lagoons near and around which grow marvelous woods; on the whole island everything is green and the foliage is like in Andalusia in April."

The islanders were delighted with the red caps, the glass beads, and the little

ships were beached and the hulls cleaned. Meanwhile Columbus heard the Indians talking about *Cubanacan*; according to the friendly interpreters from Guanahaní, gold could be found there in

abundance. In the local language *Cubanacan* meant "in the middle of Cuba," but to Columbus it sounded like "Cublaikan" or "Kubla Khan." China, at last!

The Admiral sent a delegation to find the Great Khan. It was led by Rodrigo de Jerez: he had once met an African king in Guinea, so presumably he knew the proper etiquette for dealing with an oriental ruler. Luis de Torres was the interpreter: since he knew Hebrew and Chaldaic, Columbus assumed (or hoped!) he would be able to communicate with the

Chinese. The two men were guided to a village of huts and welcomed by a "cacique," the native word for chief or leader. They did not see the Great Khan, and they found no evidence of his city with

its 10,000 stone houses that Marco Polo had described; nonetheless they were warmly welcomed by "the most important people in the village who carried them in their arms to the main house." As far as gold was concerned, there were only rumors. On the island of Babeque, the delegation was told, the natives dug it up at night on the beaches. This news was duly reported to Columbus; on November 21, Martín Alonso Pinzón and the *Pinta* secretly and without permission sailed off in search of Babeque.

Columbus stayed on Guanahaní for only two days. Then, with six Tainos aboard, he went to look for other lands which the natives told him, through gestures, lay to the south and to the west. He reached other islands in the Bahamas which

metal falconry bells that Columbus distributed generously. They also talked about another, larger island – Cuba. The Spanish squadron arrived there on October 28th, and proceeded to the cove at Puerto Gibara on the northern coast, where the

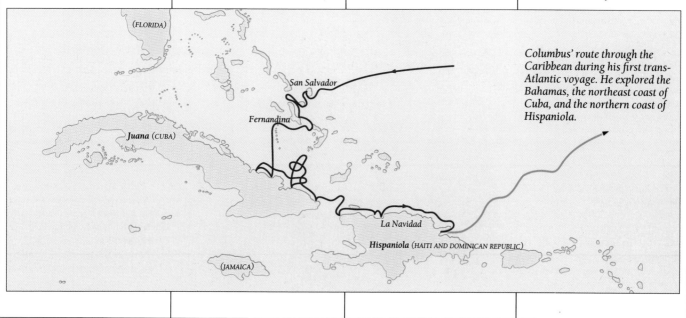

Columbus' route through the Caribbean during his first trans-Atlantic voyage. He explored the Bahamas, the northeast coast of Cuba, and the northern coast of Hispaniola.

A World of Surprises

•

*Columbus' impressions of the Caribbean's natural beauty * New discoveries: corn, tobacco, and hammocks*

One of the surprising botanical novelties was tobacco, which the natives smoked. In his logbook, Columbus describes how natives on San Salvador offered him some tobacco leaves as a gift. Pictured here is a small tobacco plant from a 16th-century botanical treatise.

Columbus' men were impressed by the variety and abundance of Caribbean parrots. One of the colorful birds they saw was the green-winged macaw (Ara chloroptera), shown here in an illustration from Prévost and Lemaire's Natural History of Exotic Birds *(Paris, 1879).*

Caribbean Coral

Columbus' first landfall was San Salvador (Watling), an island about 13 miles long (21 km) and almost completely surrounded by coral reefs, except for a two-mile (3-km) stretch to the west.

The coral reefs in the Caribbean were formed by colonies of madrepores, invertebrates of the anthozoan class that inhabit equatorial waters. The madrepores remove calcium carbonate from sea water and deposit it in crystalline forms known as coral. Reefs are only found in shallow, sunlit waters no more than 60–100 ft (20–30 m) deep.

The reefs off San Salvador are extensive and very dangerous for ships. It is a tribute to Columbus' maritime skill that he was able to find a safe passage through these treacherous, uncharted waters and bring his ships safely to anchor near the shore.

On December 5, Columbus arrived at the southeasternmost tip of Cuba, which he named Juana in honor of Ferdinand and Isabella's daughter. He named the cape Alpha and Omega. As Las Casas explains it, Columbus meant that this point marked Asia's beginning (approached from the east) and end (approached from the west). In reality, Columbus did not know for certain where he was. He still thought he was somewhere near China, in the Indies; and because of this misconception, he called the natives "Indians." This was the name given in error to these people who, according to Pietro Martire d'Anghiera, "seem to live simply and innocently in the Golden Age of which ancient writers speak so often."

At one point while exploring Cuba, Columbus and his men "lay on the grass near springs, amidst the perfume of flowers, which was extraodinary, and the sweet song of so many gorgeous little birds, in the shade of palm trees, so tall and beautiful that they were a wonder to behold." This account was written by the priest Andrés Bernáldez, who based it on the Admiral's own words (Columbus was his house guest in 1496). Truly, this new world must have seemed like a paradise to Columbus and his crew, filled with marvelous and unfamiliar sights. Even the palm trees – royal palms, unlike anything in Europe – were "a wonder to behold." (The image of Caribbean beaches lined with wind-bent coconut palms is a modern one: coconut palms did not grow there in Columbus' time.)

Columbus had hoped to find an abundance of gold and spices in the new world, but there were few signs of either in those first few days.

Still, there were other notable discoveries which in the years to come had a great social, economic, and cultural impact. The local tribes introduced Columbus to new food sources: sweet potatoes and *yuca* (or manioc), important parts of the Caribbean diet. (Another important tuber, the potato, was not discovered until the 16th century, when Spanish explorers first came in contact with the farming population of the Andes.)

Even more important was the discovery of corn or maize, which Columbus first thought was a kind of millet or barley. Pietro Martire d'Anghiera describes it as a pointed cob about a hand's breadth long and "about as thick as a forearm. The kernels, which are very evenly spaced by nature, resemble peas in their shape and size." However, he also considers it to be "a type of millet similar to that which exists in great quantities in the area around Milan and in Andalusia." Fernando Columbus, in his biography of his father, uses the native American name by which this plant became known in Europe: he describes it as "another grain like millet, which they call *mahiz*, with a very good taste when baked, roasted or pounded into flour."

Another new-world revelation was tobacco, which was unknown in Europe until Columbus' first voyage. "Tobacco" is an Arawakan word which

A Hot Commodity

Pepper was one of the highly prized spices Columbus hoped to bring back from his voyage to "Asia." He thought he had found it when he came across what he calls axi. In his History of the Indies, *Oviedo refers to it as* asci *and says it "is a rather well known plant in all of these islands and on the mainland of the Indies, and is quite common and necessary to the Indians, because this is their pepper. They always eat some of it with fish and with their other dishes. And it is not less pleasing to Christian taste." The pepper in question was actually ground red chili* (Capsicum annum); *it was different from anything known in Europe and, in Oviedo's opinion, "asci is better with meat and fish than the honest pepper; and already it is being brought to Spain."*

referred not to the plant but to the cigar made by rolling up its leaves. On October 15, only the third day in American waters, while crossing the strait between Santa Maria (Rum Cay) and Fernandina (Long Island), Columbus met a solitary islander who had in his canoe "some dried leaves, which must be greatly valued by those people, since already on San Salvador they had given me some as a gift." Later, on Cuba, Luis de Torres and Rodrigo de Jerez returned from their unsuccessful search for the Great Khan and told about "having found along the way many people, men and women, who were returning to their villages with a firebrand in their hand and herbs whose fumigations

Above, a 16th-century Venetian illustration of a hammock. It seems unnaturally stiff; probably the artist had never seen one of these new-world contraptions, and was working from a description.

they take, as they are accustomed to do." In other words, the Indians liked to smoke tobacco, which Oviedo calls "a very bad custom."

In those first weeks in the tropics, another discovery was made on Fernandina Island, in the Antilles. Perhaps it was not a great discovery, but it was one for which all later generations of sailors were grateful. As Columbus describes it in his logbook (October 17), "the sailors who went to get water told me that they had gone into the [natives'] houses which were perfectly swept and clean inside, and that their beds were similar to nets made out of cotton." These were hammocks – another American word and invention. Oviedo recognized their potential: he argues that if soldiers used hammocks, not as many would die "as now die from sleeping on the ground."

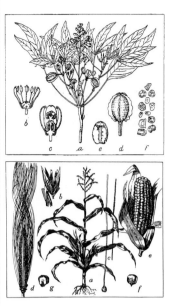

Above, two botanical drawings of important plants discovered by Columbus during his first days in the Caribbean corn, which the Indians called maize, and manioc. This last plant produces a tuber that the Indians called yuca. The tubers were grated on rough stones. The pulp was then squeezed through a bag made of woven strips of tree bark, a process designed to get rid of poisonous juices. The pulp was then made into cakes which were baked on terracotta dishes. Oviedo says that the cakes kept for a long time, and that the juice, even though poisonous, was used for beverages after being boiled two or three times.

Below, the hammock, an Indian invention that Europeans later adopted, in an engraving by De Bry.

At Last, Gold!
·
The natives tell Columbus about a native king who has "piles of gold" * On Hispaniola, Columbus finds more evidence of treasure * Columbus believes he has reached Asia

A native American ornament fashioned out of gold in the shape of a butterfly. Influenced by Marco Polo's tales and by his own memories of Guinea, Columbus was convinced that he would find gold in the "Indies;" he thought success was near when he reached Hispaniola.

In the second half of the 15th century, Portuguese explorers found large quantities of gold in Africa. Columbus undoubtedly saw some of this treasure with his own eyes when he visited the Portuguese fort – La Mina – during his voyage to Guinea in 1482 or 1483, and it must have made a lasting impression on him.

Later, when Columbus was trying to persuade Isabella and Ferdinand to finance his voyage, the subject of gold was an important part of his sales pitch. According to Oviedo, "he made many offers of great riches and estates for the royal Crown of Castile." He must have cut a strange figure in his "poor, threadbare cloak," and it is not surprising that some sceptics "considered him to be a big talker and hard to believe." But the Spanish rulers had just concluded a long and costly war. They needed money, and must have envied the Portuguese

Below, the island of Hispaniola, which today consists of Haiti and the Dominican Republic. Columbus arrived here after visiting some of the Bahamas and part of Cuba.

Below, the northwestern coast of Hispaniola, east of present-day Pointe du Cheval Blanc, in a cartographic sketch made by Columbus himself. The word "natività" marks the spot where 39 crew members remained after the shipwreck of the Santa Maria.

king, whose caravels returned from Africa laden with treasure.

Once he arrived in the New World, Columbus immediately started looking

for the "great riches" he had promised his sponsors. The first encouraging sign came on Saturday, October 13. "I was paying attention" to a group of Indians, writes Columbus, "and I was trying to understand if they had any gold, and I saw that some of them wore a little piece of it, threaded through a hole in the nose, and by means of gestures I made out that to the south, around the other side of island, there was a king who had large pots and big piles of gold."

What the Tainos really intended to communicate "through gestures" will never be known! But Columbus

At right, the landing on Hispaniola, as imagined in an engraving from De Bry.

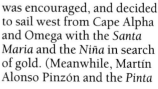

was encouraged, and decided to sail west from Cape Alpha and Omega with the *Santa Maria* and the *Niña* in search of gold. (Meanwhile, Martín Alonso Pinzón and the *Pinta*

Giovanna the Iguana

Fernando Columbus wrote a biography of his father that was first printed in Venice in 1571. In it, he tells how the Admiral's men saw a "snake" while exploring the shores of a lake on Fernandina Island (Long Island). It was about seven feet long (21.3m). With "a certain amount of fear and admiration at its ferocity and ugly appearance," they killed it with their pikes. Later on they learned that "it has a very white meat, with a very soft and pleasant taste, and it is called Giovanna by the Indians." The creature described here was an iguana, a scaly reptile that was among the strangest, most peculiar "new" animals seen during the voyage. The word "giovanna" (pronounced "jo-VAN-na") is used in the first edition of Fernando Columbus' book, but this could be a misprint or a bizarre transcription of the Indian word iguana. ("Iguana" sounds like the Spanish name "Juana," which a translator may have converted into the equivalent Italian name, "Giovanna.") Writing about this strange creature, Oviedo is "in doubt as to whether it is meat or fish, because it goes equally on the rivers and through the trees; therefore at one time I think that I should place it with the animals of the earth, and at another, to list it with the aquatic creatures."

Compared to present-day maps of Hispaniola, the early map pictured below is almost unrecognizable. Hispaniola was the first Spanish colony in the New World; it is about one-sixth the size of the country – Spain – after which it was named.

Below, a gold statuette, another ancient example of American goldsmith's art, believed to depict a cacique or chief.

had gone off on their own treasure hunt and nobody knew where they were.)

On December 6, Columbus dropped anchor in Puerto Maria, in the extreme northwest part of present-day Haiti. The island was extensively cultivated, more than the others visited so far, and well tended. It seemed to be densely inhabited; there were many villages, and the caciques or chieftains were respected leaders whose

smallest gestures were promptly obeyed. Columbus' logbook makes frequent comparisons between this island and Spain. The fields remind him of the Cordovan countryside in May; he sees trees – ilex, oaks and arbutus – like the ones in Spain; the mountains are like those in Castile; the temperature is like April in Castile, and the rain and cold are reminiscent of October in Castile. He was so impressed with the similarities that he named this new island *La Isola Española* or Hispaniola, "the Spanish Island."

As he sailed along the western coast of Hispaniola, Columbus saw more and more evidence of gold. He met local chiefs who wore objects made of wrought gold, some of which they gave to the Spaniards as gifts. When Columbus asked where the gold came from, they pointed to the interior of the island and said "*Cibao*." Columbus immediately

concluded that *Cibao* was the same as Cipango: "Among other places where they say you can find gold," he wrote, "they talk about Cipango which they call Cibao." What an exhilarating – and, in retrospect, heartbreaking –

moment this must have been. Cipango was Marco Polo's name for Japan, and Columbus must have thought that here at last was proof that he had reached Asia.

Two more precious pieces of American gold craftmanship. The statuette above was presented to the Spanish regent, Maria Cristina, by the republic of Colombia 400 years after the Admiral's return from the first voyage to the New World. Most of the gold objects brought back to Europe by Columbus and later by the Spanish conquistadores have been lost or were melted down.

The Wreck of the Santa Maria

·

*The flagship goes aground on a coral reef, and is destroyed * The first European colony, Navidad, is founded on Hispaniola*

An Indian paddling a canoe, from Navigations and Voyages, a famous collection of texts about American explorations by Giovanni Battista Ramusio (1550–1606).

On December 24, according to Columbus' logbook, "there was a dead calm" and "the sea was as still as water in a bowl." But on that quiet tropical night, disaster struck.

At dawn on December 24, Columbus had put out to sea from the Gulf of St. Thomas (Baie de l'Acul), the best harbor he had seen so far, with the *Santa Maria* and the *Niña*. (Martín Alonso Pinzón and the *Pinta* were still missing.) They were on their way to visit the cacique or chieftain Guacanagarì, who had invited the Europeans to his village and had presented them with a gold belt as a sign of friendship. By nightfall they had not traveled many miles. The *Niña* was in the lead, her sails shining in the moonlight; the *Santa Maria* followed. At 11:00 p.m. the Admiral went to bed. Juan de la Cosa, the ship's owner and at that moment the officer on duty, also went off to sleep. The senior seaman, who should have taken his turn at the helm, followed suit and the only one left at the tiller was the ship's boy, whose job was simply to turn over the sandglass every half hour.

All this was against regulations. No one was left to command the ship, which gently drifted onto the coral reefs. The Admiral was

Below, building a settlement, with a reference to Navidad, the first European settlement in the New World. This wood engraving appeared in one of the earliest printed versions of Columbus' letter to Gabriel Sanchez.

awakened. He ordered his men to put an anchor into one of the launches and to drop it some distance away; once this was done, the ship could be pulled off the reef by hauling on the anchor line. But Juan de la Cosa and his men panicked: instead of obeying Columbus' orders, they rowed frantically towards the *Niña*. The *Niña*'s captain, Vicente Yañez

Columbus' Calendar

The identity of Columbus' first landfall after crossing the Atlantic is still a subject for debate, but the date is universally acknowledged to have been October 12, 1492 – the date recorded in the Admiral's log. However, in 1492 Europeans were still using the Julian calendar, which was different from the Gregorian calendar used today. The Julian calendar's year was eleven minutes and fifteen seconds shorter than the solar year; and even though 3 extra leap years were added every 400 years, the Julian calendar in Columbus' day lagged behind the solar year. The change in calendar resulted in a 10-day difference between the dates used by Columbus and by us (Gregorian calendar). According to his logbook, Columbus set sail from Spain on August 3, arrived in the New World on October 12, and abandoned the Santa Maria on the night of December 24. But using modern dates, these events occurred 10 days later. This book cites the Julian dates used at the time; to convert them, add 10 days.

Pinzón, drove them back. But precious time had been lost. The waves had turned the *Santa Maria* sideways, and the currents drove her hull repeatedly against the coral reef. Columbus tried to make the ship lighter and higher in the water by cutting away the mainmast, but it was to no avail. The *Santa Maria* split open, and sank.

The exact location of the shipwreck is unknown, although it was probably in the vicinity of present-day Cap-Haïtien, in Haiti. All we can say is that it must have been very near Guacanagarì's village, for the cacique arrived at the scene in time to help salvage the contents and timber of the wrecked vessel.

Columbus' first problem was to figure out what to do

Above, the beautiful Indian woman seduces the knight. This is how an 18th-century Venetian print interprets the romantic relationship between Americans and Europeans at the time of the discovery.

A reconstruction of the Santa Maria, *looking toward the bow. She was the first European ship wrecked on Caribbean reefs.*

with the survivors of the *Santa Maria*. The *Pinta* was still missing, and there was not nearly enough room on the *Niña*, the smallest ship in the squadron, for the *Santa Maria*'s crew. In the end, he decided to leave 39 men behind to establish a colony

he called "Navidad" – the first attempt to establish a European settlement in America since Viking days. Two days after the catastrophe, Columbus was already interpreting it as a divine sign: "he understood that Our Lord had made the ship wreck here, so that a colony might be formed . In reality it was not a disaster, but great good fortune."

At left, De Bry's picture of Indians using fire to hollow out a pirogue, a canoe made from a single tree trunk. At right, an Indian woman with banana leaves; from Oviedo's History of the Indies (1526).

The First Colonists

According to Fernando Columbus, at least some of the first 39 Europeans who stayed on American soil were volunteers: "Many presented themselves to [the Admiral], saying that they would willingly stay there and would make their home in that land."

Fernando goes on to explain that his father left them so that "they might engage in trade and inform themselves about the country and the people, learning that language and gaining familiarity with the people: so that when he returned from Castile with help, he would have someone to guide him in all that would then be needed to populate and dominate the land." In short, they were to be in the vanguard of Caribbean colonization.

Some of their names are known. Diego de Arana, cousin of Columbus' mistress, was appointed leader. His lieutenants were Pedro Gutierrez, an officer on the Santa Maria, and Rodrigo de Escobedo, who drew up the proclamation claiming Guanahaní for the Spanish sovereigns. Also included were Master Juan, a shipwright, and Jacome el Rico, ship's boy on the Santa Maria and like Columbus a native of Genoa. Finally, there was a surgeon, a barrel-maker, an artilleryman, and a tailor; all the rest were seamen.

1493
The Return Voyage
·

*The first armed conflict between natives and the Europeans * The voyage back * A storm in the Azores almost destroys the expedition * The battered ships arrive in Portugal*

On January 6, after an absence of six-and-a-half weeks, the *Pinta* reappeared. (She had left the rest of the squadron in Cuban waters on November 21). Her captain, Martín Alonso Pinzón, claimed that it was never his intention to abandon the Admiral. Columbus pretended to believe him, but in his log he wrote that Pinzón had deserted the *Santa Maria* and the *Niña* "out of a spirit of arrogance and greed." Probably because of this situation, Columbus decided to return to Spain as soon as possible.

But before then, on January 13, a sinister drama took place in Samana Bay (Haiti). A native, his face painted black and his long hair enclosed in a kind of net of parrot feathers, had been seen on shore and brought aboard. Columbus, who had heard local stories of

Map showing route with dates: Cuba, Hispaniola, 16 January, points 17, 18, 19, 20, 21, 22, 23, 24, 25, 26. Label: "Leaves northeast trade wind zone"

feathers at the back of their heads." The Spaniards began to negotiate a trade, and had

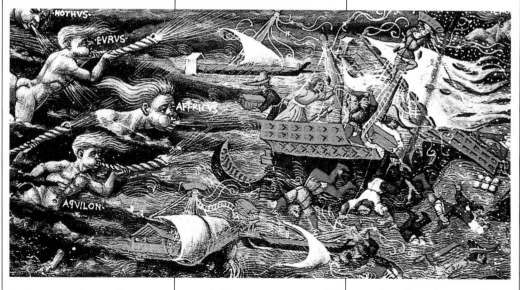

In this picture, four winds – Notus, Eurus, Affricus and Aquilon – stir up the sea and torment the ships. Bad weather at the very end of his voyage nearly spelled disaster for Columbus, but his two little caravels, although small and frail by modern standards, were strong enough to survive two fearful storms.

cannibalism, was convinced that he was "one of those Caribs who eat people." Later, seven sailors went ashore with the "Carib" and met 50 of his fellow tribesmen, all armed with bows and arrows and "wearing tufts of parrot

purchased two bows before an argument broke out. The natives rushed to the attack, but the sailors "inflicted a large wound on the buttocks of one Indian and wounded another in the chest with an arrow." The Caribs took flight. The first clash between

the peoples of the two worlds had taken place; peace between them had lasted only a month. On being informed about what had happened, Columbus said that "on the one hand, he felt regret and on the other hand, not, because the Indians should be afraid of Christians."

On January 16, the return voyage began. He set a course of "Northeast by East" (about 56°), thinking to avoid the prevailing trade winds that had carried him to the New World. The nautical strategy was perfect. The route taken by Columbus on both legs of his first voyage remained the course followed by future generations of sailors until the Age of Sail came to a close in the 19th century.

On February 3, after observing the height of the North Star, the Admiral judged that they were on the same parallel as Cape St. Vincent in Portugal. He set an easterly course, probably with the intention of passing south of the Azores: as the

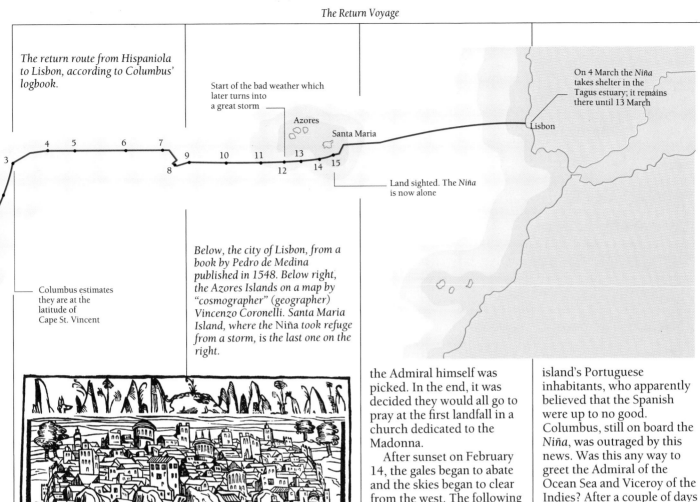

The return route from Hispaniola to Lisbon, according to Columbus' logbook.

Start of the bad weather which later turns into a great storm

Azores

Santa Maria

On 4 March the *Niña* takes shelter in the Tagus estuary; it remains there until 13 March

Lisbon

Land sighted. The *Niña* is now alone

Columbus estimates they are at the latitude of Cape St. Vincent

Below, the city of Lisbon, from a book by Pedro de Medina published in 1548. Below right, the Azores Islands on a map by "cosmographer" (geographer) Vincenzo Coronelli. Santa Maria Island, where the Niña *took refuge from a storm, is the last one on the right.*

commander of a Spanish expedition, he preferred to avoid these islands under Portuguese rule.

The weather cooperated until February 12, when the two ships were sailing precisely to the south of the Azores. That same day it began to get rough. By the night of February 13, Columbus wrote, he found himself in the middle of a storm. Unable to hold course with her sails reefed, the *Niña* "began to run before the wind, going wherever it carried her." The *Pinta* did the same and disappeared from sight.

It was a desperate

situation, and the crew of the *Niña* prepared for the worst. They threw a cask overboard; inside was a parchment telling about their discoveries, which they hoped would be found if the ships perished. They also agreed that if God delivered them from this storm, one of them would make a pilgrimage of thanks to the sanctuary of Santa Maria of Guadalupe (with a five-pound candle!), to Santa Maria of Loreto, and to the church of Santa Clara in Moguer. Three times they drew lots, taking chickpeas out of a cap, to see who would fulfill this vow. Twice

the Admiral himself was picked. In the end, it was decided they would all go to pray at the first landfall in a church dedicated to the Madonna.

After sunset on February 14, the gales began to abate and the skies began to clear from the west. The following morning they sighted land. The next three days were spent battling the winds and searching for a sheltered harbor; at last, on the morning of February 18, they dropped anchor off the island of Santa Maria in the Azores. The next morning, half of the *Niña*'s crew went ashore to carry out their penitential vow at a nearby chapel; but they were arrested by the

island's Portuguese inhabitants, who apparently believed that the Spanish were up to no good. Columbus, still on board the *Niña*, was outraged by this news. Was this any way to greet the Admiral of the Ocean Sea and Viceroy of the Indies? After a couple of days of negotiations, Columbus succeeded in obtaining the release of his crew, and they resumed the last leg of their journey on February 24th.

The final miles were among the most difficult of the entire voyage. On March 4, the *Niña* managed to limp up the Tagus estuary and anchored a few miles from Lisbon, the capital of Portugal.

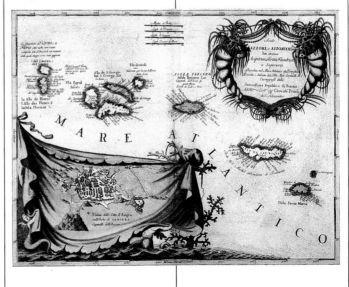

The Triumphant Return

·

*Columbus tells the King of Portugal of his discoveries * He returns to Spain, and is hailed by the Spanish court*

A 17th-century tapestry depicting Columbus at the royal audience in Barcelona. "Their Catholic Majesties received him in public," writes Fernando Columbus, "in all their majesty and grandeur, seated on a magnificent throne under a canopy of gold brocade."

Soon after the battered *Niña* dropped anchor in the Tagus estuary, the captain of a large Portuguese warship asked permission to come on board. Through sheer coincidence, that captain was none other than Bartolomeo Diaz, the great Portuguese navigator who first discovered the Cape of Good Hope and rounded the tip of Africa. The news of Columbus' discovery soon spread throughout Lisbon, as curiosity seekers and dignitaries buzzed to and from the *Niña*.

On March 9, Columbus made his way to the Portuguese court of King João II. He was accompanied by the first native Americans to set foot in Europe – proof positive, in case anyone doubted his story, that he had reached new lands. The meeting must have been a triumphant moment for Columbus, and a bitter experience for King João, who some years earlier had refused to sponsor the Admiral's voyage. João had missed one of history's great opportunities; and while publicly he put on a good face, it is said that in private the King beat his chest and called himself *hombre de mal conocimiento* – "a man of bad understanding." During the conversation, King João apparently suggested that the new lands were within the latitudes granted to Portugal by papal decree, but Columbus literally refused to give ground.

During his brief stay in Lisbon, Columbus sent to the Spanish court the famous letter in which he described his discoveries. It was dispatched to Gabriel Sanchez by land, who took it to Ferdinand and Isabella, and Columbus soon followed by sea.

On March 13, no doubt with a sigh of relief, Columbus left Portugal and the *Niña* set sail again for Spain. Finally, at noon on March 15, 1493, Christopher Columbus entered the harbor of Palos, where 32 weeks before he had commenced his great voyage of discovery.

After pausing at the monastery of La Rábida, Columbus went on to Seville for the rites of Holy Week. On Easter Sunday he received

At left, The "Virgin of the Navigators," preserved in the Alcazar in Seville. Beneath the protective mantle of the Madonna are, among others, King Ferdinand of Aragon, Christopher Columbus, Vicente Yañez Pinzón (Captain of the Niña) and Amerigo Vespucci. After returning from his first voyage, Columbus landed in Palos; from there he went to Seville to take part in the Holy Week rites.

a royal summons to appear at court. He set off for Barcelona, through Cordova and Valencia, preceded by Indians with painted faces, bearing strange new plants and parrots and (of course!) gold.

At last, before Ferdinand and Isabella in the royal palace in Barcelona, Columbus had his moment of glory. Never in his life would he know its equal. The sovereigns listened to his tale, then gave him their hands to be kissed. In the royal chapel, the *Te deum laudamus* was sung, and the sceptics who a few years before had scoffed at Columbus' plan now hailed his achievement.

But there was one man, Martín Alonso Pinzón, the captain of the *Pinta*, who did not join in the celebration.

Above, according to popular tradition, recorded here in a print by De Bry, some sceptics suggested to Columbus that the discovery of America was no great feat. In response, Columbus challenged them to balance an egg upright on the table. They all failed; Columbus then succeeded by crushing one end and resting it on the flat part. His point: difficult things seem easy after they are done.

After being separated from the *Niña* by bad weather in the Azores, the *Pinta* had made its own way to Bayona, on the northwest coast of Spain. Pinzón sent a cross-country letter to Isabella and Ferdinand requesting a royal audience; clearly, he hoped to be the first one to tell them the news (and to get the credit for the discoveries). But the sovereigns spurned Pinzón's request; they preferred to wait and listen to Columbus' account. Pinzón then sailed on to Palos, where he experienced the burning disappointment of seeing the *Niña*, which had arrived only a few hours earlier, already in port. He shut himself up in his house and a few days later he died, a great sailor but a very unlucky man.

Columbus' success entitled him to a noble title and a coat of arms (which he altered several times). Of the two pictured here, the one on the left is in the monastery of La Rábida and the other is in the Codex of Privileges in Genoa. The latter has the golden castle of Castile on a red field and the lion rampant of León; in the lower left are the islands and, to the right, gold anchors on a blue field; in the point, the family colors: a blue band on a gold field below a red stripe.

Above, native Americans at the court in Barcelona; detail of a painting by Ricardo Balaca. Isabella saw to it that the six Tainos who had come to Spain were instructed in the Catholic faith and baptized.

Good News Travels Fast

The sovereigns of Castile and Aragon received the news from Columbus himself. So did the King of Portugal. Others heard it "through the grapevine," and it is not surprising that the news traveled quickest to Italy, Columbus' native land.

On April 9, 1493 a merchant wrote from Barcelona to his brother in Milan, telling him of the discovery. He in turn informed the ambassador of Ferrara. Through this network, a message was sent on April 21 to Duke Ercole d'Este, who was eager to hear the latest geographical news. Soon the news was known in Venice, the seafaring city whose government had the best information system of the era. From Venice, the ambassador from Milan informed his lord, Ludovico il Moro. By the end of April, the news had also spread to Florence and Rome, and by June – only a few months after the original was received by Isabella and Ferdinand – a Latin translation of Columbus' "Letter" was printed in Rome.

The following year (1494), printed editions of the famous letter appeared in Paris, Basle, and Antwerp; in 1497, a German edition was printed in Strasbourg. In England, which thanks to John Cabot was the first country to follow Spain's example of looking for a western route to the Orient, the news arrived in March of 1496.

On the basis of Columbus' "Letter," most people concluded that the new lands were part of Asia. But not the Portuguese: whereas the Spanish referred to the new islands as the "Indies," the Portuguese called them Las Antilhas. *Perhaps it was a case of sour grapes, but as far as they were concerned Columbus had discovered nothing more than a new chain of islands in an old, familiar ocean.*

The Great Fleet

·

Preparations for the second voyage begin ∗ A great flotilla is assembled ∗ Equipment and supplies ∗ The fleet sets sail from Spain

Gentlemen on horseback, and infantrymen with breastplates and firearms, embarking on the great fleet bound for the Indies. From an 18th-century Venetian print.

The task of equipping the new expedition was entrusted to a committee headed by Don Juan Rodriguez de Fonseca, Archdeacon of Seville. The Admiral later complained about their work. He blamed them for supplying wine casks made from unseasoned wood: in the heat of the tropics, the wine leaked out into the bilge. He claimed that they showed him splendid thoroughbreds on parade, but supplied him with second-rate nags at the wharf. In truth the organizing effort was accomplished with surprising speed, and the Spanish threw themselves into the new "Indian" adventure with passionate

I n their letter of March 30, 1493, Ferdinand and Isabella addressed Columbus by his new titles: he was called Admiral of the Ocean Sea, Viceroy and Governor of the islands "that he discovered in the Indies." Soon, they were urging the consolidate their gains as quickly as possible.

On May 20, Columbus received his appointment as commander of a new fleet.

The city of Seville and the harbor on the Guadalquivir, in a 16th-century painting.

zeal. The crew, which numbered at least 1,200 men, included seamen, missionaries, civil servants, settlers, and assorted fortune hunters. It was the largest fleet Columbus ever commanded.

Only 28 weeks after the *Niña* returned from her first voyage, the new fleet weighed anchor in the Bay of

Admiral-Viceroy-Governor to undertake a new expedition immediately in order to extend the discoveries, colonize Hispaniola, and convert the natives to Christianity. The Portuguese were already contesting Spanish claims to the new lands, and Isabella and Ferdinand wanted to

At right, the letter that Isabella addressed to Columbus on September 5, 1493, advising him to take with him on the second voyage "a good astrologer" – that is, someone familiar with the movement of the stars and planets.

Cadiz. It was the end of September, somewhat later in the season than the first departure. In a festive atmosphere, the crews returned the salutes of the crowd assembled on land, and Venetian galleys, newly arrived from England, ceremoniously escorted the flotilla towards the open sea.

Seville Harbor

The role played by Seville in the preparations for Columbus' second voyage marked the beginning of a new era for this strategically located Spanish city. It subsequently became the home port for most New World expeditions. Her Casa de Contratación – a sort of licensing bureau – regulated the flow of men and goods between the two sides of the Atlantic. The Sevillan monopoly, which lasted until 1718, allowed for efficient collection of the "quinto," a royal tax on the unloading of goods and precious metals. Guzmán de Alfarache, *a late-16th-century Spanish novel, mentions that when* "the fleet was late arriving from America, the city was fairly short of funds."

The fleet that sailed from the Bay of Cadiz in September 1493 included, as can be seen below, three carracks, twelve square-rigged caravels, and two lateen-rigged caravels. The three carracks were named the Colina, the Gallega, *and the* Santa Maria. *The latter, which is better known* as the Mariagalante, *was the flagship of the second voyage; it was apparently twice the tonnage of the first* Santa Maria *which perished in the Caribbean.*

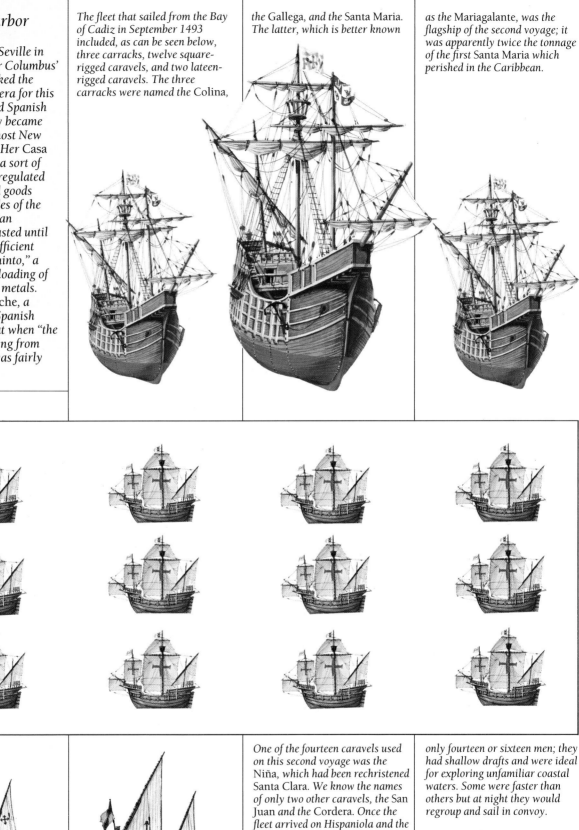

One of the fourteen caravels used on this second voyage was the Niña, *which had been rechristened* Santa Clara. *We know the names of only two other caravels, the* San Juan *and the* Cordera. *Once the fleet arrived on Hispaniola and the colonists had settled in the newly founded city, La Isabela, Columbus took the* Niña, *the* San Juan, *and the* Cordera *to explore Cuba and Jamaica. We know that they were small, with crews of* only fourteen or sixteen men; they had shallow drafts and were ideal for exploring unfamiliar coastal waters. Some were faster than others but at night they would regroup and sail in convoy.

The Cannibals of Guadalupe

·

*The fleet reaches the Caribbean * New discoveries: tropical forests and cannibals * The battle between natives and Europeans*

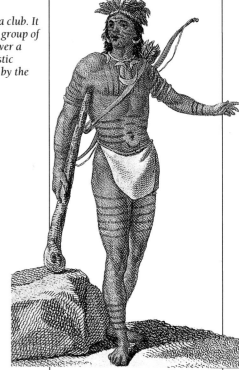

A Carib, with a bow and a club. It was on Guadalupe that a group of sailors happened to discover a village of these cannibalistic natives, so greatly feared by the Tainos.

Columbus' second crossing was quick and uneventful. As before, he stopped over at the Canary Islands; there, in San Sebastián de la Gomera, he was greeted with joyful cannonades by Beatríz de Bobadilla. The ships took on citrus fruit and vegetable seeds, mares, sheep, goats, and pigs – the Old World's botanical and zoological contribution to the future New World colony. On October 13, beyond the island of Hierro, the fleet picked up the trade wind. Columbus set a more southerly course than on his first voyage; he was aiming for the unexplored islands he had been told about on Hispaniola. The fleet sped along before strong and steady winds, and on November 2, after twenty-one days at sea, they sighted land. They had reached the islands of the Lesser Antilles: Dominica, Desirade, Maria Galante, and Guadalupe. This last island Columbus had actually christened Santa Maria de Guadalupe, fulfilling the vow he had made to the Virgin Mary after his first voyage, when his ships were spared during the huge storm in the Azores.

During the next two weeks, as they sailed

Below, the arc traced by Columbus through the Caribbean islands during the second voyage, from Dominica (bottom right) to Hispaniola (on the left), in a detail of a map taken from a book by Abraham Ortelius (1570). On this second voyage, Columbus' fleet took a more southerly course across the Atlantic in order to find the islands Columbus had heard about but not discovered during the first voyage.

northwest towards familiar Hispaniola, the crews were amazed by the variety of splendid scenery and the natural beauty of the islands. On Guadalupe, they discovered a magnificent waterfall; according to fleet surgeon Alvarez Chanca, "it was the finest thing in the world to see the height from which it fell." Then ten men got lost in the tropical forest – a mysterious world of lush vegetation unlike anything the Europeans had ever encountered before. (A rescue party had looked for them in vain; but the missing men finally found their own way back to the ships, whereupon the Admiral put the squadron leader in chains for the trouble he had caused.)

In that magical Caribbean November, Columbus discovered and named some lovely islands: Santa Maria de Montserrat (Montserrat), San Martin (Nevis), San Jorge (St. Kitts), Santa Anastasia (St. Eustatius), San Cristóbal (Saba), Santa Cruz (St. Croix), the Virgin Islands (the name comes from the

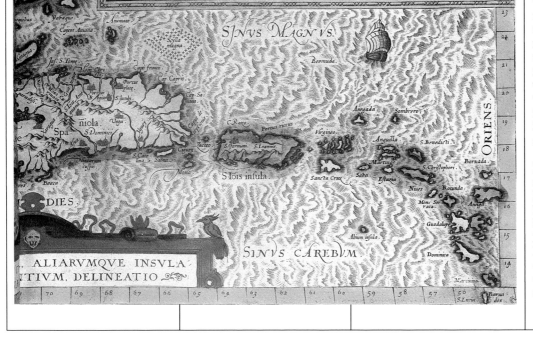

companions of Saint Ursula), and San Juan Bautista (Puerto Rico).

In the midst of this New World paradise, Columbus and his crew made a revolting and unexpected discovery. Although the logbook for Columbus' second voyage has been lost, Alvarez Chanca left a record in which he describes the Caribs or Caniba, whose "custom is bestial." These warlike people preyed on the neighboring islands, traveling up to 600 miles (965 km) in their canoes. They were armed with arrows tipped with tortoiseshell or fishbone, "and they took the women they succeeded in finding, especially the young and beautiful ones, and kept them for their own service and as maids." The Spaniards saw the cannibals on Guadalupe, or rather they saw one of their villages. Most of the Carib men had left on a raid, and the few who remained fled into the forest with their women and children. They left behind, however, some female Arawakan prisoners; according to Chanca, these captives "told us about incredible cruelties. The Caribs ate the children they had by them. They raised

only those born to mothers of their own stock. The men who are captured alive, are taken to the houses to be butchered when they are needed. The dead are eaten right away. They say that human flesh is better than anything else in the world."

On St. Croix, some thirty Spaniards landed to look for fresh water; there they freed (or captured) some Arawaks from a Carib village. While returning to the ships, they encountered a canoe full of Caribs. There were only four men and two women but they fought furiously with "poisoned" arrows, according to Pietro Martire d'Anghiera. One Carib was killed and

Cannibals, from a 16th-century woodcut.

several were wounded; the Spanish suffered two casualties, one of whom died a few days later. After the clash "there were cannibals running onto the beach in great numbers, dark skinned, fierce and terrible, painted red and other colors to increase the horror of it." This was the first real battle in the New World, and no doubt it came as rude shock to the Europeans, who probably assumed that all Indians were like the gentle, open Arawaks – peaceful folk who could be molded into faithful subjects and good Christians.

At left, the tropical forest in Guadalupe. While the fleet was stopped on the coast of this island, a party of men led by Diego Marquez became the first Europeans to enter an American jungle. Unfortunately, the men became lost; and although eventually they found their way back to the ships, Columbus threw Marquez in irons – presumably, to teach him that greater caution was needed in exploring this unfamiliar terrain.

A romantic representation of the Caribs, a tribe indigenous to the Lesser Antilles. On his first voyage, Columbus had heard stories about the Caribs or Caniba (from which we get our word "cannibal"). The Caribs were from a different stock than the Tainos whom he had met in the Bahamas and on Hispaniola. At one point, Columbus thought that the Caribs might be warriors in the service of the Great Khan of China.

1494
The Settlement of La Isabela
·
*The destruction of Navidad * The founding
of a new colony, La Isabela, on the island
of Hispaniola*

A s he drew closer to Navidad, the Admiral seemed to grow more and more impatient. He did not loiter in beautiful Puerto Rico, his latest discovery: he was eager to be reunited with the men left in Navidad at the end of the first voyage, and to find out how much gold they had discovered.

But tragedy, not triumph,

Above, in this illustration, from a 16th-century work by Antonio de Herrera y Tordesillas, natives with bows and arrows attack and burn Navidad, the colony founded during Columbus' first voyage. Participants in the second voyage blamed Caonabó, a local cacique, for the massacre; but they were only reporting what Guacanagarì, a rival chieftain, told them.

greeted the new Viceroy and Governor when he arrived at Navidad: all the colonists were dead. Perhaps some had fallen victim several months earlier to illness and the unaccustomed tropical climate, or had been been slain by their own comrades in disputes over Indian women or gold. The rest were

killed by Caonabó, a local cacique or cheftain, who had fallen upon them from the mountains and destroyed the settlement.

Columbus' friend Guacanagarì, who had moved to a village farther away, sent for the Spaniards saying that he had been wounded in the defense of Navidad. Dr. Chanca examined him, but found no wounds or scars. The Spaniards decided it was a sham: Guacanagarì was trying to avoid blame for the

slaughter. In spite of his fake wounds, however, there was no evidence that Guacanagarì was guilty of taking part in the colony's destruction. Nevertheless, the Benedictine monk Bernardo Boil urged Columbus to punish the chieftain, but the Admiral decided that this would be unwise. He ordered the dead to be buried, and then set sail again – this time in search of Cibao, a place he had heard about during his first voyage. The Tainos had told him that gold was plentiful in Cibao, so it seemed an ideal site for a

At left, Guacanagarì visiting Navidad soon after the settlement was founded; another illustration from Herrera's work. After the massacre, Guacanagarì – who was probably afraid of being blamed for what happened – claimed that he had been wounded in the defense of Navidad, but Columbus' men did not believe him.

A map of Hispaniola, believed to have been drawn by Bartolomeo Columbus, an accomplished map-maker. Bartolomeo, who had tried to drum up support in England after Ferdinand and Isabella initially refused to support his brother's first voyage, reached this Caribbean island in 1494 in command of three caravels carrying new settlers.

new settlement – a much better place than Navidad, which had been chosen not by design but as a result of the wreck of the *Santa Maria*.

To reach Cibao, Columbus had to sail along the coastline of Hispaniola towards the east, a course that took him into the trade wind. From Navidad, he proceeded first to Monte Cristi, thirty miles (48 km) to the east. Then he set sail for Puerto Plata, now a city in the Dominican Republic. Columbus had been there during his first voyage, and he described it in his logbook as "a gulf, with the most beautiful and flourishing land in the world," protected by a mountain chain at the foot of which "there is an excellent harbor." The Admiral had "thought that there ought to be an abundance of good rivers and gold there," but now, on this second voyage, he was thwarted in his efforts to return to Puerto Plata. For 25 days his fleet battled the trade winds, tacking back and forth by day without making much headway, and heaving to at night in order to avoid the reefs so common in those dangerous waters. At the end of this time, the fleet had covered only 37 miles (60 km). "The winds were so adverse," according to Chanca, that the difficulties were "greater than any we had encountered during the whole journey from Castile."

Finally, the Admiral was forced to stop in a poorly protected harbor, 26 miles (42 km) short of his goal. There, on January 2, 1494, on a little hill about 16 feet (5m) above sea level, he founded a settlement which he named "La Isabela." Located roughly 35 miles (56 km) from the present-day city of Santiago, the site of La Isabela, like the site of Navidad, was forced upon Columbus by circumstances beyond his control – in this case, adverse

as small as the huts we used at home for bird hunting, and they are covered with grass."

On the feast of the Epiphany (January 6), a solemn Mass was celebrated in a makeshift chapel, adorned with the crimson cloths that Queen Isabella had donated for this purpose. On that same day, Columbus sent out two reconnoitering parties – one under Alonso de Ojeda, the other under Ginés de Gorbalán – to find Cibao and its fabled goldmines. After two weeks, the explorers came back with promising news. The Admiral, who wanted to be part of any further exploration, set off on March 12 with 500 men. They traveled on foot over the coastal mountains of Hispaniola, then crossed the Vega Real plain until they reached a ridge between the Bao and Janico rivers, where Columbus ordered them to build a fort named after Saint Thomas (today it is called Fortaleza). There they found

The coast of Hispaniola, where Columbus founded La Isabela. He wanted to establish this second colony further east, but adverse trade winds prevented him from reaching his goal and forced him to settle in this unfavorable site.

picturesque scenery and – at last – gold. According to Pietro Martire d'Anghiera, the inhabitants of the region brought back particles and nuggets of gold in exchange for little bells. Within a few days, Columbus' men had amassed 22 pounds (10 kg) of the precious metal.

Below, preparing a beverage, a scene of native life (also from Benzoni's History*). Hispaniola was fertile, but the Spaniards did not come to the New World to cultivate the land; their object was to find gold. The European treasure-hunters wasted no time in exploiting the natives.*

winds. Unlike Navidad, however, the new colony was relatively large. Michele da Cuneo, a native of Savona whose report is an important source of information about the second voyage, says that "we built a hundred houses

According to Oviedo, native women ground maize "by hand in a somewhat concave stone, using another long, rounded stone ... in the same way painters usually grind their colors." The engraving above is taken from The History of the New World *by Gerolamo Benzoni (1563).*

In Search of Cathay

·

*The exploration of Cuba * The search for gold continues * Columbus mistakes Cuba for the Asian mainland * Back to Hispaniola*

On March 16, Columbus gave the order to build the fortress of Saint Thomas on Hispaniola; on March 29, he returned to the colony of La Isabela. Then, on April 24, Columbus put out to sea again with three caravels. On board Columbus' ship, the *Niña*, were Juan de la Cosa (not the same man as the owner of the *Santa Maria* from the first voyage) who later drew what many believe to be the first map of the New World; and an interpreter, a native American who had been captured on Guanahaní in October of 1492. He had been given a Spanish name – Diego Colón – and had learned to speak fluent Castilian.

During the next five months (April 24–September 29), Columbus explored the southern coast of Cuba, discovered and almost circumnavigated Jamaica, and reconnoitered the southern coast of Hispaniola. Bernáldez, who heard the Viceroy describe the voyage after his return to Spain, has left us a vivid record of the natural splendors witnessed by Columbus during this part of his second voyage. On the Cuban coast, writes Bernáldez, "the sweetest perfume wafted from the land to the sea," and Jamaica "is the most beautiful land that human eyes have ever seen."

But although Columbus was touched by the natural splendor of the Caribbean,

this was not the object of his search. He was looking all the time for a doorway to China, where according to Marco Polo "there are so many merchants and so rich and in such great numbers that they cannot be counted. And I also say to you that all the good men and women do nothing with their own hands, but they live as elegantly as if they were kings and the women as if they were angelic beings." Bernáldez later wrote that Columbus still believed he was about to discover the Indies ("*descubrir la tierra firma de las Indias*"). By now, Columbus had probably abandoned the hypothesis that Cibao was Marco Polo's Cipango (Japan), where the

emperor's palace "is covered with a gold roof, the way churches here [in Europe] are covered with lead roofs." But Columbus remained firmly convinced that he was at the edge of Asia. Now it was only a question of finding Cathay, proceeding through the Strait of Malacca, passing into the Bay of Bengal, and then reaching the Indian peninsula.

This single-minded belief seems on at least one occasion to have caused the Admiral to ignore, or even falsify, the evidence. On June 12, an astonishing scene took place in the Cuban bay that is now called Laguna de Cortés. "Seeing that the coast of Cuba extended far to the west," writes Fernando Columbus,

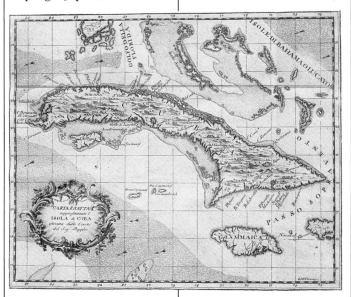

Above, a 16th-century map of Cuba. In 1494, Columbus traveled almost the entire length of its southern coast, but he did not reach the extreme western tip. Ignoring native reports, he insisted that Cuba was part of mainland Asia, rather than an island.

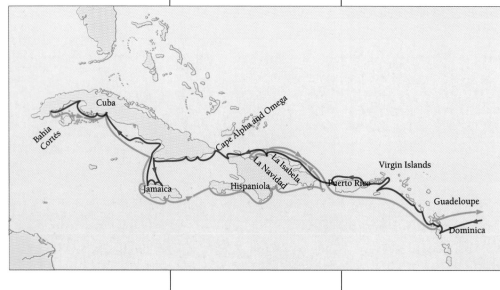

At left, Columbus' travels during the course of the second voyage, with the discovery of the Lesser Antilles – from Dominica to the Virgin Islands – and of Puerto Rico and Jamaica.

An illustration of the court of the Great Khan at Cambaluc, from a French edition of Marco Polo's story. The Venetian traveler described a world of rich and refined civilization that Columbus, after establishing the new colony of La Isabela, expected to find by sailing west from Hispaniola.

"and that sailing there was very difficult because of the countless multitude of little islands and shoals that were everywhere and since by that time provisions were beginning to run low," the Admiral decided to head back to La Isabela. But first he ordered that it be formally declared – and he had the notary Pérez de Luna put it in writing – that they were on the shore of the Asian continent. Whoever doubted it, Columbus would persuade. Whoever acknowledged it and then said the contrary would be fined almost a year's salary and have his tongue cut out. In the end, 42 men – captains, pilots and seamen – signed a declaration stating that they had reached mainland Asia. Some may have truly believed this: after all, they could not deny that the Cuban coast was much longer than any normal island, so perhaps it

was the mainland. But Columbus, it seems, knew better. Just the day before he had obtained evidence from a native that Cuba was an island. Columbus either deliberately lied to his men, or really believed he was in Asia in spite of evidence to the contrary. Perhaps it was the latter: back in Spain after his second voyage, Columbus told Pietro Martire

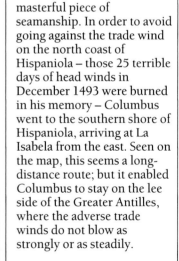

d'Anghiera that he had gone almost as far as the *Chersoneso Aureo* (in ancient geography, the name for the Malay Peninsula, near present-day Singapore).

Three and a half months after this episode, on September 29, 1494, the three caravels returned to La Isabela. From a navigational point of view, Columbus' return from the western end

of Cuba to La Isabela was a masterful piece of seamanship. In order to avoid going against the trade wind on the north coast of Hispaniola – those 25 terrible days of head winds in December 1493 were burned in his memory – Columbus went to the southern shore of Hispaniola, arriving at La Isabela from the east. Seen on the map, this seems a long-distance route; but it enabled Columbus to stay on the lee side of the Greater Antilles, where the adverse trade winds do not blow as strongly or as steadily.

On the island of Cuba. "Many people from that island came up to the ships in their canoes," says Fernando Columbus in his biography of his father, "believing that our men had come down from the sky." The natives brought "bread, water, and fish, and giving all of it happily, without asking for anything at all."

Hispaniola: A Paradise Lost

·

*The Admiral Governor * Executions and atrocities * The exploitation and enslavement of the Indians * The native revolt * The royal commission arrives to investigate * Columbus returns to Spain*

This little map of Hispaniola shows Navidad, the place where Columbus left 39 men after the shipwreck of the Santa Maria*; La Isabela, the town founded with colonists brought over on the second voyage; Saint Thomas, the fort in the interior of the island; Vega Real, the field where on March 27, 1495 the Spanish fought and defeated the Indians; the Cibao region; and Santo Domingo, the new capital that was later founded by Bartolomeo Columbus. The numbers give an idea of how the island was divided under the five caciques or chiefs: (1) Guacanagarí, (2) Behequio, (3) Caonabó, (4) Guarionex, and (5) Guayacoa.*

From the end of September 1494 until March 10, 1496, when he set a return course for Spain with the *Niña* and the *India* (the first caravel built in America), Christopher Columbus carried out his duties as Viceroy and Governor. History has delivered its verdict: during this period, the Great Navigator was a Bad Adminstrator. In his defense, it should be pointed out that Columbus was unfamiliar with the native culture, and he had been conditioned to believe that European civilization was by definition the only civilization that mattered. Today, nearly 500 years later, it is easy to find fault with the first colonial Governor; but judged by the standards of his day – the only standards he knew – did Columbus perform his duties

Hanged Spaniards, from an engraving by De Bry. Columbus resorted to capital punishment in an attempt to maintain order in the colony on Hispaniola.

as best he could? Was he well-intentioned, or (as some modern historians have argued) was he cruel and evil? Were his mistakes the product of his own character, or were they the product of his European outlook?

It is undeniable that Columbus made some serious mistakes, although it must be said that some of his errors were magnified at the time by critics at the Spanish court. His decision to leave his brother Diego in command of La Isabela while looking in vain for Cathay was a political blunder, according to later historians. (Historians are also critical of the appointment later awarded to his brother Bartolomeo, to whom the sovereigns had kindly granted three ships so that he could join Christopher with provisions and new colonists.) It is said that Diego was lacking in energy, but he cannot be blamed for all the colony's problems – among which were the settlers' difficulties in adapting to the new climate, food shortages, and illness (*buba* or syphilis).

Above, De Bry's picture of natives carried off into slavery. On February 24, 1495, the first contingent of Indian slaves left Hispaniola in four caravels. Of the 500 who embarked, 200 died before they landed in Spain. The rest were sold in Seville, but "they are not very profitable," writes Bernáldez. In the end, they fell victim to the unfamilar European climate and to European diseases.

The Admiral tried to control the Spanish colonists – Oviedo says that Columbus "had some men hanged and others flogged" in an effort to maintain discipline – but he also adopted harsh measures against the natives. Ironically, Columbus had refused to punish the Indians after the Navidad massacre, in spite of pressure from Father Boil. Now Boil was back in Spain, criticizing Columbus at court behind his back, even as the Admiral

The Island of Amazons

In 1495, during his second voyage, Columbus called again at Guadalupe. A squadron of his men explored the interior of the island; they saw no men, but captured about ten women. In his History, Fernando Columbus says that "when their children can stand on their feet and walk, [the women] give them a bow so they can learn how to shoot; and they all wear their hair long and loose about their shoulders and they do not cover any part of their bodies." One of the captives said that theirs "was a whole island of women" like "another island that they call Matrimino." Towards the end of his first voyage, on Hispaniola, the Admiral had already heard of the island Matrimino or Matinino (Martinique), which the natives said was inhabited only by women; on January 16, 1493, he had noted this in his log. Inevitably, he and his contemporaries were reminded of the Amazons, a race of warlike women who figured in Greek mythology. In describing the inhabitants of Matinino, Pietro Martire d'Anghiera said "it was believed that, at certain times of the year, the cannibals went to those women, as it was said in antiquity that the Thracians went to the Amazons on Lesbos, and that in the same way, they sent the boys to their fathers and kept the girls with them." Perhaps Columbus found only women on Guadalupe because the Carib men were elsewhere on one of their raids. But the Admiral had a different explanation. Marco Polo had written about an island called Femelle, where the women live alone except for three months of the year, when they are visited by the men of the island Malle. Columbus, who wanted to prove that he had reached Asia, no doubt believed that the island Matrimino or Matinino was the same as Marco Polo's Femelle.

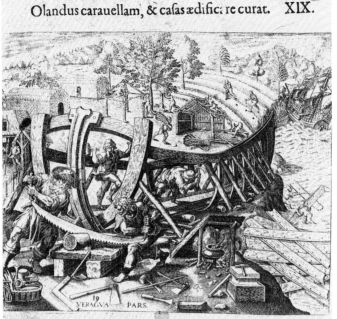

Olandus carauellam, & casas ædificare curat. XIX.

Above, building a caravel in the New World (De Bry).

adopted the brutal methods he had once advocated. On February 24, 1495, having captured 1,500 natives, Columbus sent a third of them to Spain to be sold as slaves. (He was supposed to send back gold, but more of this was ending up in the colonists' pockets than in the royal treasury. Less than a barrelful of gold had been collected up to that point.) The citizens of La Isabela were then authorized to help themselves to Indian slaves; after that, the remaining 400 natives – most of them women and children – were set free. They fled in desperation, writes Michele da Cuneo, "leaving the said children to their fate on the ground."

The natives finally revolted. Caonabó tried to form a coalition with the four other caciques on the island, but Guacanagarì refused to

Below, Indians working in the mines (from Thevet's 16th-century Universal Cosmography).

join the conspiracy and warned Columbus. Caonabó then besieged the fort of St. Thomas. The commander of the fort, Alonso de Ojeda, held out for a while, then counterattacked and captured Caonabó. Finally, on March 27, 1495, the

Spaniards won a savage and bloody battle on the Vega Real. Columbus was not a merciful victor. He demanded gold tribute from the defeated Indians. The little bells that earlier were given to the natives in friendship were transformed into instruments of oppression: every three months, decreed Columbus, each Indian was required to give him enough gold to fill one of the bells. Not surprisingly, the natives soon abandoned their villages and fled to the mountains.

At last, in October of 1495, Juan Aguado arrived with a royal commission to investigate the Viceroy. With great pomp, he and his notaries began to gather the complaints from the Spaniards who were ill, homesick, disappointed, and disaffected. Meanwhile, the rogues and bullies and fortune-seekers continued their raids on the surrounding countryside, and their atrocities against the natives.

Soon afterwards Columbus decided to return to Spain, leaving behind a devastated and ravaged Hispaniola. The pillage of the New World had begun; Hispaniola was an island paradise no more.

Dividing the World

•

*Spain and Portugal compete for the New World * The treaties of Toledo and Tordesillas * Most of the newly discovered lands are granted to Spain*

It was a fortunate coincidence for Spain that the reigning Pope at that time of the discovery, Alexander VI (at right), was a Spaniard. Previous popes gave Portugal dominion over all lands south of the Canary Islands; Alexander VI created a new east/ west division that gave Spain dominion over the Caribbean islands discovered by Columbus.

A s usually described in popular histories, there was a dramatic moment in 1493 when Pope Alexander VI, a Spaniard whose secular name was Rodrigo Borgia, coolly drew a line from north to south in the Atlantic Ocean. From that moment on, he decreed,

Below, one of the papal bulls (now in Seville) issued in the spring of 1493. At the urging of Ferdinand of Aragon and Isabella of Castile, Pope Alexander VI granted dominion over the new lands to Spain rather than to Portugal.

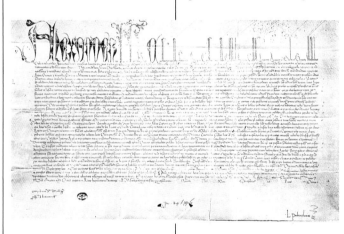

all lands discovered to the east of that line belonged to Portugal; everything to the west belonged to Spain.

Popular histories often fail to point out, however, that there already existed a division between potential Spanish and Portuguese territories. This demarcation had been spelled out in a treaty signed in Toledo in 1480: it recognized Spanish sovereignty over the Canary Islands, which at the time were not yet completely occupied; and it gave Portugal the territorial rights

to Morocco. (In point of fact, the Portuguese had established a foothold in Ceuta, at the tip of North Africa, as far back as 1415.) Moreover, the treaty prohibited Spain from sailing beyond the Canaries in search of African lands.

After Bartolomeo Diaz succeeded in rounding the southern tip of Africa, Portugal was determined to establish its exclusive right to reach the Indies by way of an eastern sea route – a right which it felt was implied in the 1480 treaty. In 1481, the

treaty of Toledo was "reinforced" by a papal bull issued by Pope Sixtus IV, which gave Portugal rights to all lands south of Hierro, the southernmost of the Spanish-ruled Canary Islands.

It is this line that both Christopher Columbus and Portugal's King João II had in mind when they faced each other in Lisbon after the Admiral returned from his first voyage. If the line of demarcation was intended to extend completely around the globe, then the lands discovered by Columbus were undoubtedly south of that line, and within the Portuguese sphere of influence. San Salvador (Watling), Juana (Cuba) and Hispaniola are in fact south

of the Canary Islands. Columbus, who brazenly told King João that Cuba was on the 42nd parallel – roughly the same latitude as New York – knew perfectly well that his new discoveries belonged to Portugal according to the existing treaty.

Below, Ferdinand of Aragon and Isabella of Castile kneeling at the feet of the Madonna, in a 15th-century painting known as the "Virgin of the Catholic Sovereigns." The decrees of Pope Alexander VI did not resolve the territorial disputes between Spain and Portugal; in the end, a compromise was reached through direct negotiations between the two powers. It left the newly discovered lands under Spanish rule.

Below, the signing of the treaty of Tordesillas (June 7, 1494) which positioned a line of demarcation 370 leagues (1,110 miles or 1,786 km) west of the Cape Verde Islands. In theory, everything west of the line belonged to Spain; everything east, to Portugal. In practice, 15th-century cartography was too primitive to determine the exact location of this line.

everything to the east belonged to Portugal. (The decree ignored the fact that the two island chains are at different longitudes, making it impossible to draw a straight north-to-south line.)

João II protested this decision, but his protests to Rome only made the situation worse. In another bull issued on September 25,

João II of Portugal, at right, from a document dated 1484. In the spring of 1493, at the end of the first return voyage, bad weather forced Columbus to land in Portugal. He was interrogated by King João, who rightly suspected that the newly discovered lands lay within the zone granted to Portugal under existing treaties.

second voyage, was sailing off the coast of Cuba.

To understand how this compromise was perceived, we should not think of the world as we know it today, but of the world as it was seen in 1494. "America" as such was unknown; it was thought that Columbus had discovered either Asian islands or a new chain of islands in the Atlantic. In either case, Portugal came out the loser: the new lands were on the Spanish side of the demarcation line. Soon afterwards Vasco da Gama rounded the Cape of Good Hope and reached Calicut on the west coast of India, thereby fulfilling Henry the Navigator's dream of finding an eastern route to Asia. But by then it was too late. The territorial lines had already been drawn, and the only consolation prize granted to Portugal in subsequent years was Brazil.

Fortunately for Columbus and his patrons, the Pope at the time was Spanish. Pope Alexander VI very quickly issued three papal bulls or decrees on May 3–4, 1493, just a few days after Isabella and Ferdinand had received Columbus on his return from the first voyage. The Pope gave Spain dominion over the lands discovered by Columbus, with the same privileges that previous popes had granted to the Portuguese in Guinea. And the third bull (*Inter Coetera*) established a line – *la raya* – that Columbus himself had proposed for dividing the world. This line lay along a meridian 100 leagues (483 km) to the west of the Azores and the Cape Verde Islands; everything west of this line belonged to Spain, and

1493 – the same day that Columbus sailed from Cadiz on his second voyage – the Pope gave the rulers of Castile and Aragon dominion over all lands discovered in the Orient, and over the "Indies" in particular.

At that point the Portuguese king, who was a close relative of Isabella and Ferdinand, decided to negotiate directly with the rulers of Castile and Aragon. The Portuguese wanted to move the line of demarcation as far to the west as possible in order to reserve for themselves some of the "Asian" lands discovered by Columbus. After much hard bargaining, the Spanish agreed to a modification of Pope Alexander VI's edict. On June 7, 1494, this agreement was ratified in the treaty of

Tordesillas, named after the city in whose royal palace it was signed. The treaty fixed the line of demarcation at a meridian located 370 leagues (1,110 miles or 1,786 km) west of the Cape Verde Islands. All this happened while Columbus, on his

This sketch shows the line of demarcation decreed by Alexander VI in his third bull (Inter Coetera), and the final demarcation established in the treaty of Tordesillas. The latter explains why Portuguese is spoken today in Brazil, which is east of the line, while Spanish is the language used in the rest of Latin America.

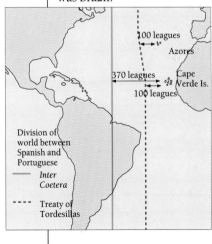

100 leagues

Azores

370 leagues

Cape
Verde Is.

100 leagues

Division of
world between
Spanish and
Portuguese

—— *Inter
Coetera*

- - - - *Treaty of
Tordesillas*

1498

The Discovery of "Another World"

•

*Columbus receives royal permission to undertake a third voyage * He lands on the coast of South America*

Columbus arrived back in Spain on June 11, 1496 with two tiny, overloaded caravels. On board were 225 Europeans, a few native Americans (the rebel Caonabó and most of the other Indians had died en route), very little gold, and a heart heavy with bitterness. Isabella and Ferdinand received him in the autumn of 1496, at which time he was

This map shows the part of Columbus' third voyage during which he discovered mainland South America in the Gulf of La Ballena, now called the Gulf of Paria, near Venezuela's Orinoco Delta.

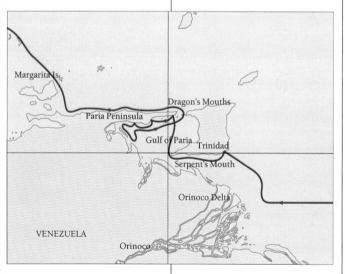

just as Vasco da Gama was arriving in India under the flag of Portugal.

On May 30, 1498, Columbus set sail from the Spanish port of Sanlúcar de Barrameda with six ships. Three of his vessels had orders to head to the Canary Islands, and from there to follow the now familiar route directly to Hispaniola. One of these three ships was commanded by

Below, Trinidad, the first new land sighted by Columbus on the third voyage. In the biography of his father, Fernando Columbus describes how the Spaniards first caught "sight of three little mountains, all together at the same moment." Because of this the island was named in honor of the Trinity, since to Columbus "it seemed that this would be pleasing to God."

Giovanni Antonio Columbus, the Admiral's cousin. With the other three ships – a carrack and two caravels – Columbus planned to cross the equator into the southern hemisphere, where according to Jaime Ferrer, a Catalan "cosmographer" and jeweler, he would find "grand and valuable things, such as precious stones, gold, herbs and spices." (In the end, however, Columbus remained north of the equator for the duration of this third voyage.)

Since the treaty of Tordesillas was now in effect, Columbus was able to undertake the crossing from the Portuguese Cape Verde Islands (at a latitude of about 15° north). The southwesterly course had taken him out of the northeast trade winds, and

reunited with his two sons, Diego and Fernando, who were royal pages. The sovereigns welcomed him kindly and graciously. Apparently, reports of Hispaniola's problems had not shaken their faith in Columbus. They proceeded to confirm the appointment of his brother Bartolomeo to

the office of *adalentado* (prefect and military governor of a province). The Admiral immediately asked for royal permission to requisition ships for a third voyage: exploration, he argued, must not be interrupted. But this time the preparations took longer; he left about 20 months later,

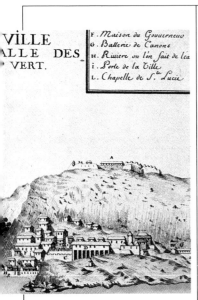

VILLE
LLE DES
VERT.

F. Maison du Gouuerneur
G. Batterie de Canons
H. Riuiere ou l'on fait de l'ea
I. Porte de la Ville
L. Chapelle de S.te Lucie

Margarita Island

As he sailed off the coast of Venezuela towards Hispaniola, Columbus passed by an island that he named Margarita, which means "pearl" in Spanish. Perhaps he called it this in homage to Princess Margarita of Austria. But the Admiral's son, Fernando Columbus, suggests another possibility in his History: perhaps "he gave it that name because of divine inspiration, since near that island lies the island of Cabagna from which an innnumerable quantity of pearls was taken." But the Admiral was unfamiliar with Cabagna when he gave Margarita its name; so if indeed he was thinking of pearls at the time, its choice was either "divine inspiration" (as Fernando says) or inspired by the "very fine, large and small strung pearls" he had seen just a few days before, worn by the women in the Gulf of Paria, on the Venezuelan coast. Columbus had asked the natives where the pearls came from; the vague directions he received corresponded roughly to the location of the island he saw a few days later and called Margarita. The pearl banks of Margarita were actually first explored by Ojeda in 1499, and in 1500 the first precious cargo was ferried away by Pero Alonso Niño.

between July 13–22 the ships slowly drifted, their sails empty, in the equatorial doldrums. This was a new and frightening experience. Moreover, in addition to the gout from which he normally suffered, the 47-year-old Columbus was now afflicted with a severe eye inflammation. When the winds picked up again, they were from the southeast rather than the northeast.

On July 31 Trinidad was sighted, and in the following two weeks Columbus encountered a bewildering sequence of new sights: unfamiliar islands, the mangrove swamps and lagoons of the Orinoco Delta in northern Venezuela, Indians of a different language and culture than those they had known before, pearls, the Venezuelan coast stretching as far as the eye could see.

Although the logbook from Columbus' third voyage

The Orinoco Delta landscape. The Admiral noted that an enormous quantity of fresh water was flowing into the ocean and he came to the correct conclusion that it could only come from a large continental land mass. Yet he persisted in thinking, or hoping, that this land mass was a hitherto unknown part of Asia.

has been lost, it is summarized in the writings of the missionary Bartolomé de Las Casas. According to Las Casas, Columbus later made this report to Isabella and Ferdinand after landing on the coast of Venezuela: "I believe that this is a very large mainland, of which, until today, we have had no knowledge … As Your Highnesses well know, very little was known about other lands other than what Ptolemy wrote. And now the truth appears, and it will appear even more: if this is mainland, then it is something extraordinary, and

Below, Margarita Island as pictured in one of De Bry's engravings.

Perlarum insula ob vnionum copiam sic dicta. XII.

ERTIA *in Indiam expeditione, Columbus sinum Pariensem ingressus, Cubaguam appulit, quam ipse Perlarum Insulam nuncupauit, quia quum eum sinum nauibus percurreret, Indos è lintre ostreas piscantes conspexit: quas edules esse rati quum aperuissent Hispani, plenas vnionibus repererunt, vnde magna illis lætitia oborta. Peruenientes ad littus in terram egrediuntur, vbi mulieres Indicas pulcerrimos vniones collo & brachijs gestantes obseruant, quos vilibus rebus redimunt.*

D   Colum-

will be so to all scientists, because the river that joins here is large enough to make a fresh water sea 48 leagues across."

On August 17, bound for Hispaniola again, Columbus reflected on what he had seen: he wondered if the immense Venezuelan river, the Orinoco, might be the one that flows from the Earthly Paradise "that everyone says is at the end of the Orient." Even though Columbus had transformed European "cosmography," part of him still believed (or wanted to believe) in the stories and legends passed down by Ptolemaic and medieval geographers.

Some years later, in 1503, Columbus wrote a letter from Jamaica in which he used the words *otro mundo,* "another world," to describe these new lands. And South America was truly another world: its discovery was the major result of the third voyage, and marked the first time since Viking days that Europeans had set foot on the mainland of either North or South America. (John Cabot may have landed in some small bay in North America in that same summer, but he never returned; there is no proof that he achieved his feat before Columbus' Venezuelan landing on August 5, 1498.)

1500
Disaster and Disgrace

•

*Columbus returns to Hispaniola, and finds the colony in shambles * Rebellion in La Isabela * A new governor arrives, arrests Columbus, and sends him back to Spain in chains*

Before returning to Spain in 1496, Columbus had given his brother Bartolomeo the job of constructing a new capital on Hispaniola. In August of the following year, Bartolomeo had carried out these instructions by founding Santo Domingo on the southern coast of the present-day Dominican Republic, not far from gold mines that the

Below, embarking for the Americas. It does not appear that there were any women among the settlers on Columbus' second voyage. Probably the first Spanish women arrived on Hispaniola on the ships sent to reinforce La Isabela in 1495.

Spaniards had recently discovered. On August 31, 1498 Columbus arrived in Santo Domingo where, according to Fernando Columbus, he hoped "to rest from the troubles endured on the [third] voyage and to find peace there among his people." Instead he found himself in the middle of a crisis.

The island had been politically torn apart by a struggle between those loyal to the Columbus family, who controlled the central and southern part of the island, and a party of rebels to the west who were loyal to Francisco Roldán, a man the Viceroy himself had made *alcalde* (mayor and magistrate) of Hispaniola.

Roldán's revolt in the isolated colony lasted two more years before Columbus was able to settle it. In the end, he capitulated to the rebels' requests: he granted each colonist a parcel of farm land, which – along with the natives who lived on it – was his to exploit. Las Casas says that "the farmers who were paid to cultivate the land and the miners – the Spaniards, that is – behaved like idlers and lived off the sweat of the

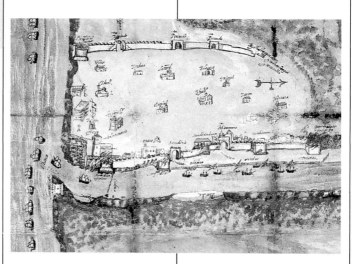

Above, the walls of Santo Domingo and the harbor in the Ozama River in a picture dating from 1616. The city, situated on the southern coast of Hispaniola, is today the capital of the Dominican Republic.

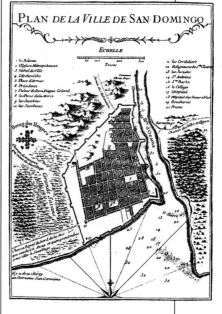

Indians, each one usurping by force three, four, ten of them to keep as servants."

Then came another blow, this time from overseas. As Oviedo describes it, "their Catholic Majesties, angered by the information they had about the way in which Don Christopher Columbus and his brother were governing this island, decided to send as governor a venerable knight, and a familiar of the court, a very honest and religious

Another view of Santo Domingo, from an 18th-century French print. Santo Domingo was founded in 1496 by Bartolomeo Columbus while his brother Christopher was in Spain after the second voyage; in later years, the city became a Spanish base for exploration and conquest. It was the point of departure for Juan Ponce de León's expedition to Puerto Rico, and for Hernan Cortez' conquest of Mexico.

At left, in the detail of a print by De Bry, the imprisoned Columbus is taken on board the ship that carried him back to Spain. In spite of this bitter ending, Columbus' third voyage was, in geographic terms, successful and important: on August 5, 1498, Columbus became the first European to set foot on mainland South America.

Viceroy. On February 13, 1502 Don Nicolas left Cadiz with 30 ships and 2,500 people – sailors, colonists, and soldiers – to supply the decimated colony with new blood. Columbus, meanwhile, was staying in a Franciscan monastery in Granada.

man." The "venerable knight" was Don Francisco de Bobadilla. He arrived in Santo Domingo on August 24, 1500. There he saw Spaniards hanging from the gallows, and heard Diego Columbus, who was in charge in the capital in his brother's absence, cheerfully tell him that some more Spaniards would be hanging up there the next day. Bobadilla promptly arrested the three Columbus brothers and sent them back to Spain in chains.

The scene of the shackled Admiral is well known. As soon as Columbus was on board, the captain of the *Gorda* offered to remove the chains, but Columbus did not want him to. Knowing "by what authority and on whose behalf [Bobadilla] had put him in irons, he did not want anyone other than Their Majesties themselves to do about this what was most pleasing to them" (Fernando Columbus, *History*). The Admiral bitterly resolved "to save these shackles as relics and as a souvenir of the reward for his many services."

It is difficult to consider this sad and humiliating episode objectively, but in the end it appears to have been motivated largely by politics and "reasons of state." A modern historian, Paolo Emilio Taviani, calls it a *coup d'état*: the crown was

undoing the curious partnership it had made with the Columbus family, having decided to manage the increasingly lucrative business in the "Indies" on its own. In some respects, the decision was an outgrowth of changes that were happening in Europe itself, where feudal relationships were beginning to give way to the bureaucratic functionings of the modern state.

Columbus and his two brothers were received by

Isabella and Ferdinand at the Alhambra in Granada on December 17, 1500. The sovereigns promised justice: they allowed the Columbus brothers to keep their titles, and to send a trusted man to Hispaniola to collect what they were owed from the island's trading and goldmining profits.

Don Nicolas de Ovando was appointed the new governor and supreme justice of the islands and mainlands, but was not given the title of

A 19th-century painting of Columbus in chains on the Gorda, the ship that carried him back to Spain at the command of Hispaniola's new governor, Don Francisco de Bobadilla. The Admiral was put in chains in Santo Domingo; the Gorda's captain later offered to remove them, but Columbus refused. Columbus kept the manacles for the rest of his life.

The Age of Discovery Continues

·

*The Portuguese reach India by sailing east
* Portugal discovers Brazil * An English
expedition reaches Newfoundland *
Spanish expeditions to South America*

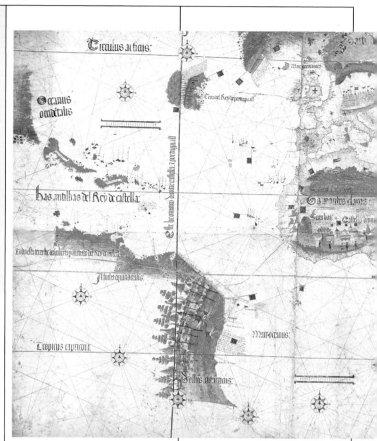

While Columbus was exploring South America and fighting for his political life in Santo Domingo, other countries were not idle. During this period the Portuguese finally arrived in (and returned from) the Orient that Columbus thought he had found on the coast of Cuba. Vasco da Gama left Portugal in July of 1497, taking the place of his father, to whom the king had given command of the expedition but who had died

At right, the "Cantino Map" (1502) shows the newly discovered lands in the Caribbean and part of South America.

before the departure. Da Gama reached and rounded the Cape of Good Hope, following the route traced by Diaz. In Malindi, on the coast of Kenya, an Indian pilot came on board. On May 20, 1498, after 23 days of monsoons, he reached Calicut on the west coast of India. Although only a

quarter of the 200 men who sailed from Portugal returned from this voyage, it was hailed – rightly so – as a very successful expedition; and it appeared that the trade routes opened up by Da

Gama could be exploited more profitably than the lands discovered by Columbus to the west. Spurred by this success, the Portuguese sent Pedro Alvares Cabral to sea on March 9, 1500 with a fleet of 13 or 14 ships. He navigated the Atlantic following da Gama's directions, but he traveled further to the west than expected and struck land 16° south of the equator, in the southern part of present-day Bahia (Brazil).

Meanwhile, an English expedition led by John Cabot made the first European landing in North America since Viking times. Little is known about Cabot except that that he was probably from Genoa, and a naturalized Venetian about the same age as Columbus. With licenses from King Henry VII of England and a

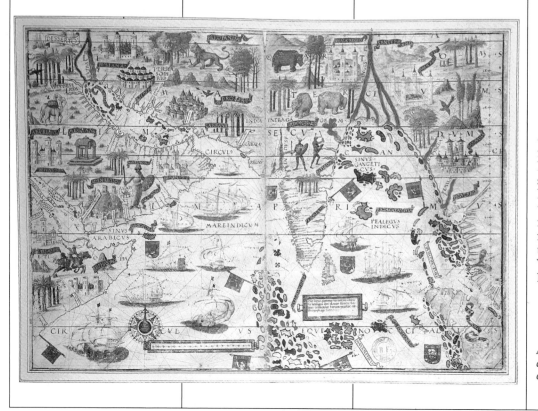

At left, India, from a 16th-century atlas dedicated to King Manuel I of Portugal.

Between 1499 and 1500 there were seven or eight Spanish expeditions. In the spring of 1499, Alonso de Ojeda, Juan de la Cosa, and Amerigo Vespucci set sail from Spain (the first two men traveled all along the coast of Venezuela as far as the Gulf of Maracaibo). In November of the same year, another expedition set forth under the command of Vicente Yañez Pinzón, a veteran of Columbus' first voyage. Pinzón crossed the Atlantic and landed near Recife, on the easternmost coast of Brazil.

These and the other voyages were already cutting into the commercial profits to which Columbus was entitled according to the terms of his original

ship, the *Mathew*, that must have been as small as the *Niña*, Cabot left Bristol in May of 1497 and landed near Cape Degrat in Newfoundland. Eleven weeks later Cabot was back in Europe and the following year, 1498, he put out to sea with five ships, one of which returned almost immediately. Of the other ships, and of Cabot, nothing more was heard.

Under Gaspar Corte Real, the Portuguese also probed the North Atlantic. In May 1501, on his second voyage in the North Atlantic, Real appears to have reached Newfoundland. Two of his three ships returned in October with tales about a cold, icy land covered with pine trees. They brought back 57 Indians, but not Real: like Cabot, the commander of the Portuguese expedition and his third ship disappeared without a trace.

During this period the Spanish were actively exploring the Caribbean and the South American coast.

The Cantino Map

Italy's Duke of Ferrara, Ercole d'Este, was curious about the New World discoveries, and sent Alberto Cantino to Lisbon with instructions to gather as much news as possible in the Portuguese capital. The so-called Cantino map, a Portuguese planisphere, is the result of these inquiries. (See illustration above left.) Cantino sent the map to the duke on November 19, 1502. In addition to the Spanish Antilles (Las Antillas del Rey de Castella), it shows the northern coast of South America which Columbus discovered in 1498 and which Ojeda further explored in 1499. Also shown is the coastline's continuation to the east and south, including Brazil, which was discovered by Cabral in 1500. According to Samuel Eliot Morison, the distinguished Columbus scholar, this is the oldest European map with America on it. Other historians give that distinction to a planisphere made by Juan de la Cosa.

agreement with the rulers of Spain. Shipowners paid all expenses, and a tenth of the profits went to the Crown, which also reserved up to one-tenth of each ship's cargo capacity for its use. The voyagers who followed in Columbus' footsteps resembled the *conquistadores* of Mexico, who later declared that their goal was to serve God and to get rich – though not always in that order. Nevertheless, in these years no great treasures were found: the expeditions returned with some pearls and small caches of gold, and most of them carried back cargoes of wood and slaves to cover expenses.

Manuel I ("the Great") succeeded his cousin King João II to the throne of Portugal in 1495. He ruled the country until his death in 1521. It was during his reign that Vasco da Gama arrived in the Indies by way of the Cape of Good Hope, and Cabral landed in Brazil.

Above, Vasco da Gama. He was very young when he led the Portuguese squadron that arrived in Calicut (India) in 1498. He commanded a second expedition to India in 1502, and was made Viceroy of India almost 20 years after his first voyage. He died there at the age of about 55.

At left, England's King Henry VII, who sponsored John Cabot's North Atlantic expedition. Cabot, an Italian born in Genoa and a citizen of Venice, was the first European since Viking times to land in North America.

1502

The Final Voyage

•

*Columbus receives approval for a fourth voyage * He plans to sail around the world * The hurricane in Hispaniola * Columbus explores the coast of Central America*

In September of 1499, Vasco da Gama reappeared in the Tagus estuary on his way back from the *real* India. Two-and-a-half years later, on March 14, 1502, Ferdinand and Isabella authorized Columbus to undertake a fourth voyage. The plan that Columbus had

Columbus organized his fourth and last expedition in little more than four weeks. The Atlantic crossing, from Grand Canary Island to St. Lucia, turned out to be the fastest one ever, up until that time. Above, a picture of the island of St. Lucia. The Admiral left Spain with four caravels, similar in size to the Niña. The flagship, whose name we do not know, was accompanied by La Gallega, *the* Santiago de Palos, *and the* Vizcaina.

At right, victims of a shipwreck, in an engraving by De Bry.

presented to the sovereigns – and which had probably been accepted, at least in part, because of da Gama's success – was an extremely ambitious one. Columbus proposed to find the Strait of Malacca (near present-day Singapore), to sail west to India, and then to return to Spain by retracing Bartolomeo Diaz' route around the tip of Africa. In other words, Columbus planned to go around the world by sailing west.

He left Spain for the final time on May 9, 1502, only three months after Don Nicolas de Ovando, the new "Governor of the Indies," was sent to Hispaniola. The Admiral was carrying with

Although Columbus warned Bobadilla that bad weather was imminent, the fleet of 30 ships set sail for Spain; shortly afterwards, all the ships but one were destroyed by a violent hurricane that no doubt resembled Pieter Bruegel's painting of The Storm *(below).*

him a courteous royal letter addressed to Vasco da Gama, just in case the two explorers met along the way. His fleet consisted of four caravels and 150 men, including his brother Bartolomeo and his second son, the 14-year-old Fernando. A rapid Atlantic crossing soon brought him into sight of the Caribbean island of St. Lucia. On June 29 he anchored off Santo Domingo, the capital of Hispaniola – this in spite of

the fact that Isabella and Ferdinand had explicitly forbidden him to land there. His intention was to exchange one of his slower caravels for one of the many ships that had crossed the Atlantic with the new governor. Not suprisingly, Ovando obeyed the royal instructions and prohibited Columbus from entering the harbor.

Columbus arrived off Santo Domingo just as a great convoy of about 30 ships was being fitted out to carry Francisco de Bobadilla and a considerable cargo of gold back to Spain. Columbus warned them not to sail because a hurricane was imminent; he then brought his own ships to a sheltered part of the island. But as the weather seemed to be fine, the Admiral's cautionary words were apparently taken as a gesture of spite: Bobadilla ignored the warning, and his fleet departed. Even before they rounded the eastern end of Hispaniola, however, a violent hurricane descended. The majority of Bobadilla's fleet sank; only a few battered ships managed to escape. Some 500 people drowned, Bobadilla among them. Only one caravel, the *Aguja*, proceeded on to Spain. Its cargo included 4,000 gold pesos earmarked for Columbus. This led some of Columbus' detractors to add sorcery to their list of criticisms: how else could the

Hurricanes

Hurricanes were among the most frightening and unexpected dangers of early Caribbean exploration. These violent storms, which normally occur between the months of June and October, are accompanied by furious rains and violent winds that sometimes reach a velocity of up to 190 miles (300 km) per hour. They last a short time, often only a few hours, but they can leave behind a trail of destruction and calamity.

The Europeans had never encountered storms of this kind, not even in the stormy North Atlantic or in their eastward forays to the Indian Ocean. The word hurricane itself is derived from a Caribbean word, hurican. They are a result of very low atmospheric pressure – a feature of all tropical climates, but particularly of the Caribbean.

Columbus witnessed the fury of these storms in October of 1495, when almost all the ships anchored off La Isabela were sunk. (There may have been an earlier experience, in September of 1494. While returning from exploring Cuba and Jamaica, bad weather – perhaps caused by a hurricane – forced the Admiral's ships to take shelter on the island of Saona.) On these occasions, Columbus' sea sense had noted the warning signs: the long, oily waves; the unusual tides; the white cirrus clouds that veiled the sky; the short gusts of wind that died down as quickly as they rose; the clear scarlet sunset. Undoubtedly he saw these same signs off the coast of Hispaniola in 1502, and thereby was able to lead his ships to safety while Bobadilla's fleet perished.

Above, the coast of Nicaragua. Columbus reached Cabo Gracias a Dios – the point on mainland Central America that separates Honduras and Nicaragua – after a difficult sail against the wind.

A Mayan stele or funerary stone. In Central America, Columbus saw natives belonging to, or influenced by, the Mayan culture. The reports speak of, for example, "a tomb on a hill as big as a house" (una sepultura en el monte grande como una casa). The occupants of the large canoe encountered on Guanaja Island were certainly Mayans. The signs of an advanced culture only confirmed Columbus' belief that he was in Marco Polo's Asia, and that nearby lay the Strait of Malacca and the Indian Ocean.

Admiral's treasure survive when everything else perished? In reality, of course, Columbus' timely warning had nothing to do with magic; in yet another demonstration of his superior seamanship, Columbus had accurately read the signs of impending bad weather.

From Santo Domingo, Columbus and his small squadron sailed past Cuba, stopping at Guanaja Island off the coast of Honduras, and then landed on the mainland of Central America. Columbus immediately proceeded to look for the strait which he was sure led from the Caribbean to the Indian Ocean. For 3–4 weeks, he slowly and painstakingly tacked eastwards; after covering 170 nautical miles (315 km), he finally reached the cape separating present-day Honduras and Nigaragua, which he named Cabo Gracias a Dios. From that point on he was able to follow the shore of Central America, which turns to the south, with greater ease.

During this period, according to Fernando Columbus (who on this voyage was an eyewitness), on Guanaja they met up with "a canoe as long as a galley and eight feet [12.9 m] wide, made completely out of a single piece of wood, and similar in shape to the others, which was loaded with goods." The cargo, and the women and children of the 25 "Indians" who manned it, were under a "canopy made out of palm leaves." These people were Mayas from the Bay of Campeche, part of the Gulf of Mexico, who were visiting their southern trade centers.

So Near, And Yet So Far

·

*Columbus believes he is on the verge of discovering a sea passage to India * He discovers gold in Panama, and attempts to establish a mining colony * The natives attack, and Columbus abandons the settlement*

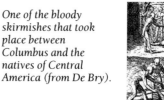

One of the bloody skirmishes that took place between Columbus and the natives of Central America (from De Bry).

There was a moment when the Admiral felt that success was at hand, that he had found the Strait of Malacca at last. It was in October of 1502, about 10 years after his first trans-Atlantic crossing, on the coast of Panama. Sheltered by islands, a passage opened between the green banks. Immediately, the turquoise waters widened promisingly. For a couple of days they explored the shore in their boats, hoping to find a way through to the "Indian Ocean." But it was an illusion; they had discovered the Lagoon of Chiriquí, measuring about 15 by 30 miles (24 by 48 km). In the background rose the mountains of the Cordillera; nearby, according to the natives with whom Columbus spoke, lay "another ocean." Columbus could taste success: he was convinced the natives were

describing the Bay of Bengal (the Indian Ocean). It would be another eleven years, however, before Vasco Nuñez de Balboa, in battle harness and brandishing his sword, would set eyes on the ocean that today we call the Pacific.

If Columbus had pressed on over the mountains and through the jungle for another 200 miles (320 km),

Pre-Columbian gold. After seeing similar artifacts in Panama, Columbus tried unsuccessfully to establish a mining settlement.

he would have found the Pacific – and history's verdict on this fourth voyage might be different. Instead, he decided to establish a settlement in Panama. Undoubtedly, his decision was influenced by the fact that he had discovered gold on the coast of Veragua (Panama): the natives, according to Fernando Columbus, were "all as naked as when they left their mother's womb; all they wore was a gold mirror around their necks." Sometimes, the people gave these gold mirrors to the Spaniards as

Landscape of the Central American coast, which Columbus discovered in 1502-1503.

gifts, sometimes they traded them for two or three little bells. Columbus concluded that Panamanian gold mines would become even more lucrative than Hispaniola's, so he decided to leave his brother Bartolomeo in command of a mining camp and to hurry back to Spain for additional resources. Dreams of treasure sent him across the Atlantic in 1492; ironically, the same dreams would keep him from finding an even greater prize ten years later – the discovery of the Pacific Ocean.

The site selected by

An Indian attack on a European ship on the American coast (also from De Bry). Native hostility thwarted Columbus' attempts to establish a settlement in Panama during his fourth voyage.

The map shows the Caribbean route followed by Columbus during his fourth voyage. Its most important aspect, from a geographical standpoint, was the exploration of the Central American coast.

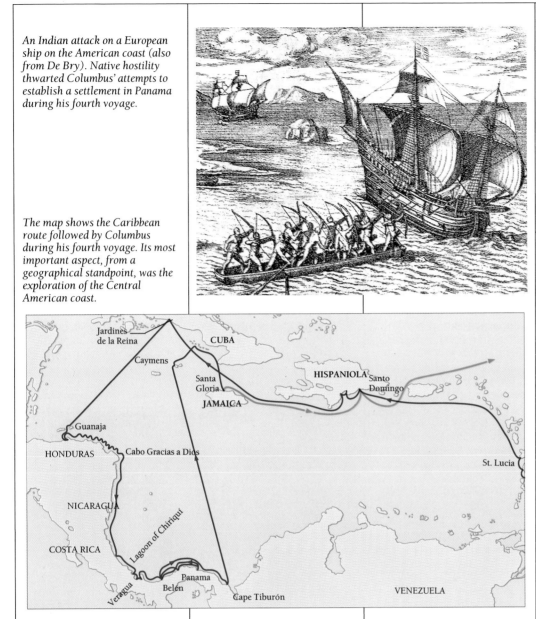

Coca

A number of pre-Columbian ceramic figures, like the one at the bottom of this page, have swollen cheeks; some historians conclude that these are representations of people chewing coca. (The word comes from the Aymara language, and originally had a completely innocent meaning – "plant.") The practice was common among Andean peoples, from Colombia to Bolivia.

A passage from Fernando Columbus' History has led some scholars to think that this custom was first noted during the course of Columbus' fourth voyage. In February of 1503, according to the Admiral's son, Bartolomeo Columbus was reconnoitering the Panamanian coast. A short distance from the mouth of the Urira River, he met a cacique accompanied by about 20 men. "While the cacique and his chiefs were there, they never stopped putting this dried herb in their mouths and chewing it, and sometimes they also put in a certain powder which they carried, along with this herb, which seems to be a very bad thing."

Columbus for the mining colony was at the mouth of a river which he named Betlem (Bethlehem, now called Belén), in honor of their arrival on the feast of the Epiphany. Eight houses roofed with palm leaves were built. But the colony was short-lived. The local cacique, named Quibián, was friendly at the outset; after he learned that the foreigners intended to stay, however, he decided to attack the Spanish ships and houses, and to massacre the inhabitants. His plans were discovered, and there followed a battle that ended with bloodshed on both sides and the taking of Indian hostages who later

committed suicide. Finally, on Easter Day (April 16, 1503), Columbus departed, leaving behind an unseaworthy ship. (Another ship was abandoned shortly thereafter for the same reason.) On May 1, having navigated almost the entire Central American coast, the Admiral set sail once more towards the open sea.

1503
Mutiny and Magic
·
*Columbus is marooned on Jamaica * The lunar eclipse * Mutiny * Rescue arrives from Hispaniola * The final return to Spain*

INDIA·MAIOR·

On Jamaica, Columbus' men waited and hoped. On the second day of the new year (1504), about half his men mutinied and tried to escape in Indian canoes. The mutineers were led by the Porras brothers; their sister's lover, the Treasurer of Castile, had forced Columbus to take them on the voyage. The rebels failed and turned back. They then kept to themselves in their own

At left, another "Indian" from a German print dated 1509.

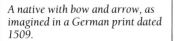

A native with bow and arrow, as imagined in a German print dated 1509.

Columbus set sail for Spain from Cape Tiburón; the northeast trade wind was off the starboard bow and, sailing close-hauled, the two surviving caravels drifted with the wind and the currents for about 100 miles (161 km). Then, writes Fernando Columbus, "we came in sight of two small, low islands, full of turtles; the sea around there was filled with them, so that they looked like little rocks." These islands were two of the Caymans, a final discovery. With great difficulty, the two ships, which by this time could barely keep afloat,

arrived in Puerto Santa Gloria, a harbor on the northern coast of Jamaica that Columbus had already seen in 1494. Columbus and his men stayed there in the beached ships for an entire year (June 25, 1503–June 28, 1504). It was a magnificent place to be shipwrecked, with its clear waters, coral reef, beautiful beach, and nearby tropical forest.

The problem of supplies was solved after Diego Méndez reached an agreement with the local natives; and in order to avoid provoking them, the Admiral ordered that no one was to stray from the boats. Columbus then tried to send a message to Hispaniola asking for help. A first attempt by Diego Méndez failed when his boat was attacked by Indians at the eastern end of the island. Then two canoes, commanded by Méndez and Bartolomeo Fieschi, each with six Spaniards and six Indians aboard, succeeded in traveling the 108 miles (175 km) to Hispaniola, with a stop at Navasa after the first 78 miles (126 km).

At right, a page from Regiomontanus' astronomical almanac, which predicted the lunar eclipse of February 29, 1504.

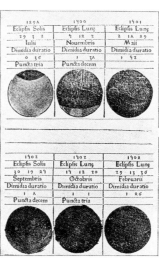

camp, but because they pillaged Indian villages, the Indians were no longer willing to bring food.

It was at this point that the Admiral worked some magic. Among the books he carried on board was the *Ephemerides astronomicae ab anno 1475 ad annum 1506* by Johann Müller, otherwise known as Regiomontanus. These astronomical charts predicted an eclipse of the moon for the night of February 29. Columbus summoned the Indian caciques and made a threatening speech about the power of God, their wickedness, the punishment that would follow, and the warning sign – i.e., a lunar eclipse – that they would

Below, Jamaica. On the northern coast, in the harbor of Santa Gloria (today called St. Ann's Bay), "the Admiral and the others who were with him stayed for a year," according to Oviedo, "sleeping and living in the caravels which lay on their sides, up to their decks in sea water, near the land."

The clash with the mutineers in Jamaica, from an engraving by De Bry.

receive. He told them to watch the moon. The eclipse came on schedule, exactly as predicted in the *Ephemerides*. According to Fernando Columbus, "their fear was so great that, with great weeping and screaming all around, they came running to the ships loaded with provisions." Columbus used the eclipse as an opportunity to measure the time

difference between Cadiz and Puerto Santa Gloria. He also tried to calculate the latitude of his position, and came within 31 miles (50 km) of fixing his exact location – a virtual bull's-eye by early-16th-century standards.

A small ship sent from Hispaniola eventually appeared, left a cask of wine and half a salt pork, and told everyone to be patient. Help would soon arrive. Meanwhile, Columbus tried to settle the dispute with the mutineers; but instead it came down to a fight. On May 19, 1504, as the natives looked on in astonishment, Bartolomeo Columbus and his loyalists defeated the

mutineers. The rebels asked for mercy, and Francisco Porras was put in irons.

Not until August 13 did the rescue ship arrive. After another month, on September 12, Columbus embarked for Spain with his brother Bartolomeo, his son Fernando, and a few other survivors. Finally, on November 7, 1504, sick and prematurely aged, the Admiral disembarked in Sanlúcar de Barrameda. He was in such ill health that he had to be carried to Seville.

An Indian pirogue or canoe, from Gerolamo Benzoni's History of the New World *(1563).*

Shipworms

The Greeks called them "worms that eat wood." The great 18th-century naturalist, Linnaeus, called them calamitas navium, *"ship's calamity." Like cockles, oysters and mussels, shipworms belong to the lamellibranch class of mollusks. There are various species of these creatures, one of which is aptly named* Teredo navalis *– literally, "ship's worm." Their bodies are very elongated and are protected by a small shell. They have two astonishing characteristics. First, they have an insatiable appetite for submerged wood, in which they dig endless tunnels. Secondly, they are amazingly fertile and prolific: one female can produce two million eggs.*

During the age of wooden ships, shipworms were a serious problem. They were very destructive, particularly in warmer tropical waters like the Caribbean. In Columbus' time, sailors tried to protect their hulls against the ravages of shipworms by frequently cleaning the hulls and caulking them with pine tar or pitch, but neither of these measures resulted in lasting protection. Not until later in the 16th century did sailors come up with something better: they covered everything below the waterline with sheets of metal, a much more effective deterrent than pitch.

These creatures did so much damage to Columbus' ships that he was forced to break off his return voyage to Spain and make an emergency landing in Jamaica. Probably he did not have any pitch on board, or he had been counting on taking aboard supplies of pitch when he reached Santo Domingo. Columbus paid a high price for not repairing his vessels sooner: two caravels had already been abandoned on the Panamanian coast because of shipworms, and the two surviving ships were soaking up water like sponges by the time they were beached in Santa Gloria Bay.

1506

The Journey's End

•

*The death of Queen Isabella * Columbus obtains little satisfaction from King Ferdinand * The Admiral's last days*

Queen Isabella of Castile died on November 26, 1504, less than three weeks after Christopher Columbus returned from his fourth and final trans-Atlantic voyage. "The world has lost its noblest ornament," wrote the courtier Pietro Martire d'Anghiera about the strong-willed queen who had continued to govern from her sickbed up until the day she died. "The Admiral made no small show of sorrow," wrote Fernando Columbus in the final pages of his father's biography, "since it was she who had supported him and favored him; and he had always found the King to be rather cold and opposed to his affairs." Perhaps this comment is unfair to King Ferdinand of Aragon: after all, Columbus'

Columbus appears here on his knees before the Virgin; behind him is St. Christopher, the patron saint of travelers.

member of the King's retinue, to press these claims at court; but Diego made little progress, and in the end Columbus decided to seek a royal audience directly with King Ferdinand.

A statue of Isabella of Castile in Granada's Royal Chapel, where she and King Ferdinand were buried. When the Queen died in November of 1504, Columbus mourned the loss of his greatest protector and patron.

voyages were undertaken with the support and patronage of both Isabella *and* Ferdinand. Nevertheless, it is significant that the "Indies" belonged to the Crown of Castile and were, technically speaking, part of Isabella's domain.

At the time of Isabella's death, Columbus was 53 years old and in bad health. He was also bitter about the way he had been treated by the Spanish sovereigns: he believed they had failed to honor the payments and privileges to which he was entitled. He urged his son Diego, who was now a

Not until May of 1505 did his health allow him to make the trip from Seville to Segovia, where Ferdinand was holding court. As a concession to his ill health, Columbus was granted special royal permission to travel by mule instead of by horse. (The use of mules as saddle animals was normally prohibited.) The King received Columbus cordially, but refused to acknowledge the validity of the Admiral's claims. However, Ferdinand did allow an arbitrator to be named. At Columbus' request, the arbitrator was Father Deza, the Franciscan who had supported him in that final crisis in 1492 and who was now Archbishop of Seville.

In financial terms, the results of this negotiation were relatively favorable to

Columbus. His right to a tenth of the proceeds from the lands he discovered was confirmed. In practice, this meant he was entitled to one-tenth of the one-fifth reserved to the Crown – in other words, two percent of the total, a very considerable royalty. Regarding his rights as "Viceroy" and "Governor" of the Indies, Columbus received no satisfaction: he was told that the King was entitled to modify or even to deprive him of these titles and privileges in the interests of the state. As a concession of sorts, Ferdinand was willing to give Columbus a property in Spain, Carrion de los Condes, and the revenues connected with it. But Columbus, furious at the King's refusal to confirm his colonial titles, was insulted by this royal offer and angrily spurned it.

Still, Columbus refused to abandon his claims. With difficulty, he followed the court to Salamanca and then to Valladolid. There, illness forced him to take to his bed. At his side were his two sons, his brother Diego, and faithful companions like Diego Méndez and Bartolomeo Fieschi. Absent were his brother Bartolomeo, who had traveled to Seville to petition Juana, the new Queen of Castile; and Beatríz, the mother of Fernando, for whom Christopher provided in his will.

Perhaps Columbus in his final days was an outmoded character, but contrary to popular legend he died

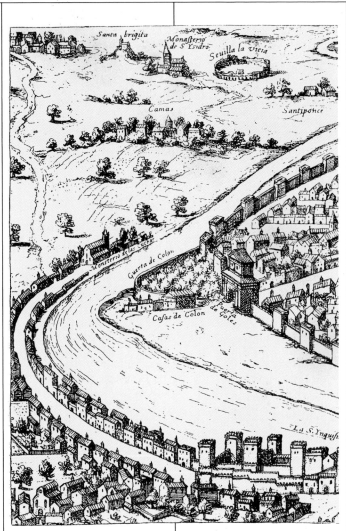

At right, the location of Columbus' house (Casas de Colon) in Seville and, on the opposite shore, the monastery of Las Cuevas where his remains were placed in 1509.

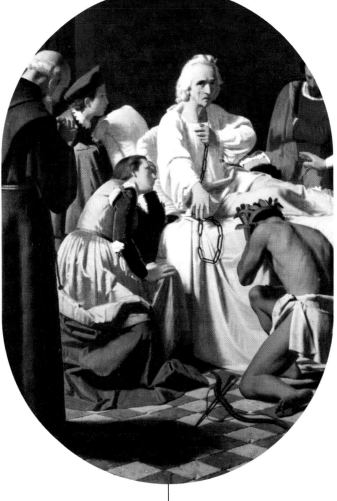

neither poor nor abandoned; in fact, he was a wealthy man. According to his son Fernando, the Admiral was also pious: on his death bed, "having first taken all the sacraments of the Church with great devotion, [he] said these final words: *in manus tuas, Domine, commendo spiritum meum.* Into your hands, O Lord, I commend my spirit." It was May 20, 1506, Ascension Day. Christopher Columbus, Admiral of the Ocean Sea, was dead, and with him ended one of the great adventures of all time.

Columbus' last moments in a painting by Luigi Sciallero. He clutches the chains from the third voyage in his hands. He wanted the shackles to be placed in his tomb, but this does not appear to have happened.

The Admiral's Sons

Christopher Columbus' two sons grew up at court. The elder, Diego, was the son of his Portuguese wife. He made an excellent marriage to Maria de Toledo, a relative of the King. In 1508, King Ferdinand made Diego the governor of Hispaniola. Diego lived in the Alcazar of Santo Domingo; he died in 1526.

His younger brother, Fernando, was the son of Beatríz, the Admiral's Cordovan lover. Fernando accompanied his father on the fourth voyage at the age of fourteen, and later returned to America with Diego. His biography of Christopher Columbus remains an important source of information for modern historians. He died in Seville in 1539.

The Lost Discoverer

•

Columbus' original burial place in Spain ∗ His remains are transported to Hispaniola ∗ The mystery of his final resting place

In the cathedral of Seville, in the transept across from the famous Patio de los Naranjos and in front of the Puerta de San Cristóbal, there is a solemn funerary monument to Christopher Columbus. On a late-Gothic-style base, four large multi-colored heralds, wearing vestments with the Spanish royal coats of arms, are carrying a bier covered with noble drapery on their shoulders. In reality, there were no representatives of the Spanish Crown present at the Admiral's funeral in the church of Santa Maria de la Antigua in Valladolid. The monument in Seville is a 19th-century tribute, created by Arturo Melida in 1892, the fourth centennial of the discovery, for the cathedral in Havana. It was brought to Spain in 1899 when Cuba gained its independence from Spain. It is very unlikely that the monument contains the Admiral's remains. Their final resting place, like many other aspects of Columbus' life, is clouded by uncertainty.

Christopher Columbus' funerary monument in the cathedral in Seville. It is doubtful that the lovely 19th-century tomb contains the Admiral's mortal remains. The large figures supporting the bier are emblazoned with the coat of arms of the late-15th-century Spanish kingdoms.

What is known is that Columbus was originally buried in the cloisters of San Francisco in Valladolid; three years later, his remains were transferred to the monastery of Las Cuevas in Seville. After several decades – probably sometime between 1537–1559, according to modern historian Paolo Emilio Taviani – the Admiral made a fifth and probably

final voyage across the Atlantic. His bones were laid to rest in Santo Domingo on Hispaniola, along with the remains of his brother Bartolomeo, his son Diego, his grandson Don Luis, and his great-grandson Don Cristóbal.

Centuries passed. Then, in 1795, the Treaty of Basle temporarily transformed Santo Domingo into a French possession. The Duke of Veragua, a direct descendent of Columbus, thought it unseemly that the remains of his famous ancestor should remain in French hands. He wanted Columbus disinterred and the remains transported to Spanish soil. After further inquiry, however, he was told that the external signs identifying the burial place had been removed in 1655, when the

At right, the monument to Columbus in the cathedral of Santa Maria in Santo Domingo. Diego Columbus, the navigator's son, laid the cathedral's first stone in 1514, and later had his father's remains transported from Spain and buried here.

inhabitants of Santo Domingo feared that the city would be attacked and pillaged by the English. But some human remains – presumably, the Admiral's – were found in a tomb near the main altar, and in 1795 were transported to the cathedral in Havana. (These were the same remains that were then brought to Seville in 1899, after Cuba became independent of Spain.).

But were these bones really the Admiral's? The question created an uproar in 1877 when the presbytery of the cathedral of Santo Domingo was being enlarged. During the construction, Monsignor Rocco Cocchia, the Apostolic Delegate in Santo Domingo, found the coffins of the Admiral and of his grandson Don Luis. He concluded that the remains of Don Diego, rather than of his father, must have been transferred to Havana in 1795 – either through error or at the wish of the Dominicans, in whose care the church was entrusted at that time. As Morison describes it, there ensued "a disgusting controversy," with the prelates of Santo Domingo being accused of fraud and forgery.

The coffin that Cocchia discovered had three inscriptions, one on the lid, another carved in lead on the inside of the lid, the third on a silver plate that was found in the bottom. They were examined by an expert in 1891, who concluded that they were very old. The first one was a cryptic abbreviation: "D. de la A. P.er A.te." Perhaps this stands for *Descubridor de la America Primer Almirante* – that is, "Discoverer of America, First

At right, a bronze and crystal urn preserved in Genoa; it contains some of Columbus' ashes, brought back from Santo Domingo in 1878. At the same time, small amounts of his ashes were sent to Venezuela and to the Italian city of Pavia.

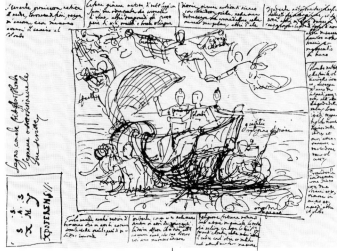

Admiral." The "First Admiral" part makes sense: the title "Admiral of the Ocean Sea," the only one of Columbus' "rights" never questioned, had been regularly transmitted to his descendants. But "Discoverer of America" causes some hesitation. The Spanish spoke of the Indies, rather than of America, between 1537 and 1559, when Columbus' body was carried across the ocean and, in accordance with his son Diego's wishes, laid to rest in Santo Domingo. It is hypothesized that the word "America" was supplied by a German or a Flemish craftsman: there were plenty of both in Spain at that time. If this explanation is correct, then the tomb discovered in Santo Domingo was truly the Admiral's, and all of his remains lie there except for

some ashes which, in 1878, were transported to a bronze shrine in his native Genoa, to Pavia (Italy), and to Venezuela.

Two of the greatest Columbus scholars, Taviani and Morison, are convinced that Columbus' remains were never moved from Santo Domingo. Others think that his bones were transported from Santo Domingo to Havana in 1795, and from there to Seville in 1899. And it has been argued by some that his remains have been in the monastery of Las Cuevas since 1509, or in Valladolid, or even in Puerto Rico.

Perhaps the final answer to this puzzle will never be known with certainty, and the Admiral's final resting place – like his birthplace – will remain a mystery forever.

At left, Columbus sits in a floating chariot, with Providence at his side. Perhaps this is the sketch for an allegorical painting honoring the Admiral. It is the work of an unknown 16th-century artist, who may have obtained approval of the sketch from Columbus himself. (His monogram can be seen in the box to the left.)

Below, an allegory showing the discovery of the New World; from a ceremonial shield belonging to Charles V, King of Spain and Holy Roman Emperor from 1519–1556.

A Saint or Sinner?

His contemporaries agree that Columbus was a man of intense religious faith, especially devoted to Mary and to Saint Francis. Some 300 years later, these qualities captured the imagination of Don Giovanni Maria Mastai Ferretti, who was then secretary to the Apostolic Legate in Chile and later became Pope Pius IX. Ferretti was a great admirer of Columbus; according to his religious view of history, Columbus was an instrument of Divine Providence who introduced the Gospel to heathen natives on the other side of the Atlantic. In 1622, the Church had canonized the Jesuit missionary Francis Xavier, who had devoted his life to evangelical work in the Orient; but the Church still lacked a comparable symbol of New-World evangelization. In Ferretti's opinion, Columbus was deserving of this honor; and in 1866, Ferretti (now Pope Pius IX) initiated the proceedings that would lead, he hoped, to the Admiral's beatification – the first step towards sainthood.

But like the titles conferred on Columbus during his lifetime, this one was problematic. First, the process was interrupted when the Holy Father indignantly shut himself up in the Vatican after Italian troops entered Rome. The issue was reopened in 1891, and a vote finally taken, during the reign of Pope Leo XIII (1878–1903). In the end, however, there was only one vote in favor of beatification. Others, apparently, felt that Columbus was more sinner than saint. Weighing against him was the fact that he had an "illicit" relationship with Beatríz de Arana, the mother of biographer Fernando Columbus; and that in 1495, as Viceroy on Hispaniola, he had sent 500 captured natives back to Spain to be sold as slaves.

1507

Amerigo, America

·

*The voyages of Amerigo Vespucci * His exploration of the South American coast on behalf of Portugal * How the New World came to be named after him*

A portrait of Amerigo Vespucci. The inscription on the frame identifies him as the "discoverer of Brazil" (Terrae Bresilianae Inventor). He was born in Florence, and began his career in the commercial establishment of Lorenzo di Pierfrancesco de' Medici, on whose behalf he was sent to Seville in 1491. He stayed there for several years in the service of Giannotto Berardi and then, in 1495, he became head of a "branch office."

A gold wasp on a blue band in a red field: this was the coat of arms of the Vespuccis, a prominent Florentine family. In Columbus' day, the Vespucci name conjured up images of the beautiful Simonetta, who married into the family and died at the age of 26, probably from tuberculosis. Her portrait was wonderfully drawn by Piero di Cosimo, and she may have been the model for two of Sandro Botticelli's greatest paintings, *Primavera* (Spring) and *The Birth of Venus*. In later centuries, however, it was another Vespucci – her cousin Amerigo – who achieved lasting fame and immortality of sorts.

Over the years, there have been various explanations of how America got its name. One French scholar, for instance, maintained that Columbus encountered the word "America" during his fourth voyage, when he thought he heard it used as the name of a Nicaraguan tribe and a chain of mountains. But such explanations are spurious. The fact is, as everyone knows, that "America" was named after Amerigo Vespucci.

To many people this seems the final injustice that history has inflicted on Columbus. Be that as it may, Vespucci was not directly responsible for robbing the Admiral of this honor. Columbus knew him and held him in high regard. Vespucci helped requisition supplies for the Admiral's third voyage; and

in a letter addressed to his son Diego and written in the last days of his life, Columbus calls Vespucci "a very fine man." He was also an explorer in his own right who made two voyages to the New World.

First, in 1499, Vespucci was the "cosmographer" or geographer in an expedition led by Alonso de Ojeda, a veteran of Columbus' second voyage. In Guiana, several ships under Vespucci's command proceeded southeast along the coast of South America, where they discovered the Amazon River. His second voyage was undertaken with Gonçalo Coelho on behalf of Portugal, which according to the treaty of Tordesillas "owned" Brazil and the eastern part of South America. In June of 1501, in the Cape Verde Islands, Coelho and Vespucci met up with the Portuguese explorer Cabral. They crossed the Atlantic to Brazil, and at Porto Seguro (today Baia

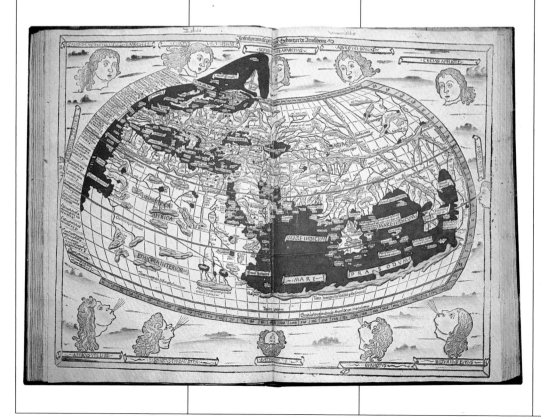

In his Geografia, *Ptolemy identifies only three continents. But in this 16th-century map, a fourth land mass has been added. The map was prepared in the monastery of Saint-Dié in Lorraine, where the geographer Waldseemüller wrote his work crediting Amerigo Vespucci with the discovery of a "fourth part of the world," which he called "America."*

Cabralia, about 200 miles or 320 km south of Salvador), they picked up two men who had been left there by Cabral the year before. On New Year's Day of 1502, the ships entered the bay of Guanabara; they named it Rio de Janeiro to commemorate the day of its discovery. It is not clear how much further south Vespucci and Coelho pushed, although it is possible they proceeded as far as 52° south, the latitude of the Falkland Islands.

They returned to Portugal in September of 1502. By then, Columbus had already departed on his fourth

Below, an engraving based on a drawing by Giovanni Stradano; it is an allegory of Amerigo Vespucci's discoveries. "America" is a shapely girl waking up and rising from her hammock; wild animals roam among the trees; and, in the background, the natives are roasting human flesh. The drawing was made in 1521 – the same year that Magellan, sailing westward, finally arrived in Asia. Magellan's feat was accomplished nine years after Vespucci's death, and fifteen years after Columbus died.

The above engraving, from De Bry, shows Amerigo Vespucci in Brazil. "We found the whole land to be inhabited by completely naked people," wrote Vespucci, "and they live according to nature."

elaborate play on words. But the phrase was picked up by other geographers in Lorraine, who in turn passed it on to the great Flemish cartographers of the late 16th century. Thanks to their maps, the name stuck.

So it was that History delivered the Admiral one final, ironic blow: the man who, in his lifetime, was erroneously credited with the discovery of Asia and the Indies was in the end deprived of an honor he truly deserved.

voyage. As a result, the Admiral had no idea that the South American coast, which he himself had discovered on his previous voyage, extended so far. Had he known this, he might have been less hopeful of finding a passage through the Central American isthmus and into the "Indian Ocean."

Around the time of Vespucci's return to Portugal, there appeared several popular little books filled with adventurous tales about the New World. They were partially based on authentic letters of Vespucci, but for the most part they are pure fabrication. But the books were attributed to Vespucci and, rightly or wrongly, they contributed to his fame.

One of these spurious stories appears in geographer

Martin Waldseemüller's *Introduction to Geography* (*Cosmographie Introductio*), published in Lorraine (now part of France) a year after Columbus' death. This same work contains a passage that may explain why today we refer to "America" instead of "Colombia." Waldseemüller speaks about a fourth part of the world, over and above the three Ptolemaic parts: "*et quarta orbis pars (quam quia Americus invenit) Amerigem quasi Americi terram sive America nuncupare licet.* The fourth part of the world, discovered by Amerigo, could be called Amerige, almost the land of Amerigo or America."

Perhaps this suggestion was meant only as a literary flourish, and was intended as nothing more than an

Vespucci and "America," from a 1516 edition of Martin Waldseemüller's influential Cosmographie Introductio.

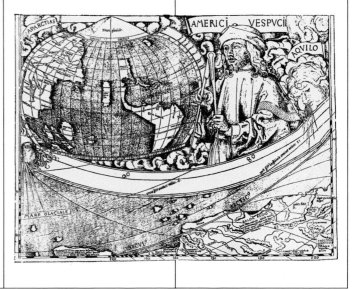

Chronology

1451
Cristoforo Colombo (Christopher Columbus) is born near Genoa, on the northeast coast of Italy. He is the son of Domenico Colombo, a weaver, and his wife Susanna Fontanarossa.

1460
Prince Henry the Navigator, who was responsible for Portugal's early voyages of discovery, dies. Portuguese navigators reach the Cape Verde Islands off the coast of West Africa.

1466
At about this time, young Columbus begins his seafaring career on board ships that sailed commercial routes between Genoa and other Mediterranean ports.

1469
Ferdinand, future King of Aragon, marries Isabella, future queen of Castile. Their marriage results in the political union of these two Spanish kingdoms.

1471
Portuguese explorers reach Guinea, on the west coast of Africa.

1475
Columbus embarks on his longest voyage to date, to the Aegean island of Khíos off the coast of modern Turkey.

1476
Columbus sails with a Genoese convoy that is attacked by French privateers. His ship is sunk, and he swims ashore to the nearby Portuguese port of Lagos.

1477
Columbus sails from Portugal to England and back.

1478
Columbus sails to the Spanish island of Madeira on a commercial expedition which ends in a legal dispute.

1479
Columbus marries Felipa Moniz Perestrello, daughter of the governor of Porto Stefano, a Spanish possession near the island of Madeira. Their son, Diego, is born there.

1480
The Portuguese explorer Ferdinand Magellan is born.

1482
Columbus sails to the Portuguese gold mine in Guinea, on the west coast of Africa.

1483/1484
Columbus urges João II, King of Portugal to approve his plan to discover Asia by sailing west. The proposal is rejected.

1485
Columbus, by now a widower, moves to Spain with his young son Diego.

1486
Columbus presents his plan to Isabella of Castile and Ferdinand of Aragon. He meets Beatríz de Arana, a cousin, by whom he has a second son (Fernando) two years later.

1487
Isabella and Ferdinand reject Columbus' plan. Bartolomeo Diaz, the Portuguese navigator, reaches the southern tip of Africa, the Cape of Good Hope.

1489
Queen Isabella meets again with Columbus, and leads him to believe that an expedition will be forthcoming once Spain's war with the Moors is concluded.

1491
Columbus, frustrated by the delays, prepares to leave Spain; at the last instant, he is summoned back by assurances from Queen Isabella.

1492
January 2: the Moors surrender to Isabella and Ferdinand. April 17: the Spanish sovereigns approve the terms under which Columbus will undertake, on behalf of Spain, to find a westerly route to Asia. In May, preparations begin in the Spanish port of Palos. August 3: Columbus' three ships – the *Niña*, *Pinta* and *Santa Maria* – set sail from Spain. October 12: Columbus completes his first Atlantic crossing and lands on a Caribbean island that he names San Salvador (now called Watling). He discovers Cuba (October 27) and Hispaniola (December 6). On Christmas day, the *Santa Maria* goes aground and sinks.

1493
January 16: Columbus begins the return voyage in the *Niña*, leaving behind colonists at a place he calls La Navidad. March 4: Columbus reaches Portugal after a tempestuous crossing. March 15: Columbus reaches Palos, the Spanish port from which he first departed. April: Columbus is greeted in triumph by the Spanish sovereigns, who authorize a second voyage. September 25: Columbus departs Spain with a flotilla of 17 ships. November: Columbus makes landfall in the Caribbean, and goes on to explore the Lesser Antilles and Puerto Rico. He returns to Navidad, the colony on Hispaniola, but finds no survivors from the first voyage.

1494
January: Columbus founds a second colony, La Isabela, on Hispaniola. He sails to Cuba, Jamaica, and back to Hispaniola.

1495
March: Columbus and his men engage in the first full-pitched battle between Europeans and native Americans. June: Columbus sails back to Spain.

1497
The Italian explorer John Cabot reaches Newfoundland.

1498
Columbus departs from Spain on a third voyage to the New World. He discovers Trinidad and South America before returning to Hispaniola, where he finds the Spanish colonists in revolt against his brother's administration. This same year, Vasco da Gama reaches India.

1499
The Italian navigator Amerigo Vespucci reaches South America.

1500
In an effort to restore order to Hispaniola, Queen Isabella and King Ferdinand send another governor to Hispaniola; Columbus is arrested and sent back to Spain in chains. This same year, the Portuguese explorer Pedro Alvarez Cabral discovers Brazil.

1501
The Spanish sovereigns agree to let Columbus undertake a fourth voyage; his plan is to circumnavigate the world. Columbus leaves Spain in April, and after escaping a hurricane in Hispaniola he explores the Central American coast. Vespucci explores the coast of South America and discovers the Rio de la Plata.

1503
Columbus' attempts to establish a gold-mining camp in Panama are thwarted by hostile natives. He and his men are shipwrecked on Jamaica, where they remain for a year awaiting rescue.

1504
Queen Isabella of Castile dies. A ship sent from Hispaniola rescues Columbus and his men from Jamaica. Columbus embarks for Spain in September, where he arrives in bad health.

1505
Columbus has an audience with King Ferdinand, who refuses to confirm the Admiral's rights and titles.

On May 20th, Christopher Columbus, Admiral of the Ocean Sea, dies in Valladolid (Spain).

Picture Sources

*Americans, in an engraving from
the beginning of the 16th century
(from an edition of* Mundus
Novus, *one of the writings
attributed to Amerigo Vespucci).*